Deafness in Society

Deafness in Society

Jeffrey E. Nash
Macalester College
Anedith Nash
University of Minnesota

LexingtonBooks
D.C. Heath and Company
Lexington, Massachusetts
Toronto

Library of Congress Cataloging in Publication Data

Nash, Jeffrey E.
    Deafness in society.

    Bibliography: p.
    Includes index.
    1. Deaf. 2. Deafness–Psychological aspects. I. Nash, Anedith.
II. Title.
HV2380.N33   305   81-3753
ISBN 0–669–04590–x   AACR2

Copyright © 1981 by D.C. Heath and Company

Published simultaneously in Canada

Printed in the United States of America

International Standard Book Number: 0-669-04590-x

Library of Congress Catalog Card Number: 81-3753

Contents

List of Figures
and Tables

Foreword

More than most physically handicapped, the deaf have remained hidden. We notice the posture and the hesitant gait of the lame; we see the wheelchair of the paraplegic; we observe the guide dog or white cane of the blind. Not so with the deaf. Their loss of hearing is almost entirely invisible to the average person. Even the muted signs used in public may pass unnoticed to those outside the deaf world.

This hidden character of the deaf world has spawned many myths, not only about deafness but also about the deaf themselves. Social scientists have not always escaped these popular misconceptions—the stereotypes created by the hearing. Indeed, misconceptions continue to be expressed in scientific journals and scholarly books. One of the major reasons that professionals do not escape these cultural stereotypes is linguistic ignorance. Anthropologists have long known that the first rule for studying another culture is to learn the language. When social scientists have studied the world of deafness without a working knowledge of sign language, they often only confirm their stereotypes.

In this book Jeffrey Nash and Anedith Nash unravel the inner workings of deaf culture and society. They also show how the world of the deaf can only be understood in relation to the larger American society. Their work has grown out of more than a decade of intensive fieldwork and analysis. Using the native language, Ameslan, as well as understanding the variant forms sign language has taken, they have conducted interviews and observed the social world of the deaf. In addition to studying communication among the deaf, they have examined the many points where the deaf world intersects with the hearing world. This book is rich in ethnographic data that reveals the insider's perspective on deafness and adapting to deafness in a hearing society.

But this study is more than merely an ethnographic description. I believe it breaks new ground in two important ways. First, the authors combine the theoretical and methodological approaches of ethnography, ethnomethodology, and functional analysis. They begin by carefully laying out the premises of these three strategies for understanding social life. Then they do an effective job of making use of all three in an integrated fashion to help us take off the cultural blinders that block a valid understanding of the deaf.

Second, the authors have drawn on linguistics, sociology, and anthropology to construct a theory of deafness. This theory and its assumptions are spelled out in a progressive manner throughout the book and culminate in chapter 7 with the concept the authors term "adaptation as a function of framed interpretations." They show how and why individuals choose to adapt in one way or another to deafness in the context of a hearing society. In doing so, the authors have broken new ground in a sociological understanding of deafness. Their analysis also will generate numerous hypotheses that will lead to additional research and refinement of their adaptional theory.

I believe the greatest need of professional scholars in the field of deafness, of educators and practitioners who work with the deaf, and of the hearing lay person as well is a deeper understanding of deafness. We need to understand at a fundamental level that deafness is far more than loss of hearing. Deafness is a social and cultural condition. The shared meanings of deafness held by the deaf often contrast with the meanings held by the hearing. This book goes a long way toward making clear this social nature of deafness in the context of American society.

James P. Spradley
Macalester College

Acknowledgments

We have profited from the criticism and contributions of many scholars who read portions of this book as it was being developed. Bill Stokoe showed an early interest in our effort. Harold Finestone offered helpful reminders of the power of Merton's theoretical writings. Irwin Rinder kindly read the adaptations chapter, and his encouragement was timely and effective. We owe a special thanks to Jim Spradley, who urged us to continue this project. Finally—but not insignificantly—Peggy Stivers diligently, intelligently, and graciously typed the manuscript. Of course, we stand solely responsible for any misrepresentation of what it means to be deaf and for any undue liberties we may have taken with the conceptual language of sociological analysis.

Deafness in Society

1

Deafness in Sociological Perspective

C. Wright Mills (1959, pp. 6-8) wrote that the sociological imagination must attend to three interrelated questions: What is the structure of the particular society being studied? Where does that society stand in human history? In it, what varieties of men and women prevail? Although the society of people who cannot hear is certainly small, and not all persons with a hearing loss belong to it, all three of Mills's concerns are pertinent to an understanding of deafness. The experiences of deafness have their own social organization. This structure stands in relation to the history and trends of the larger hearing society, and we can identify the varieties of people who make up this society. The various chapters in this book are exercises in a version of the sociological imagination applied to a group of people that is difficult to define, elusive of observation, and little appreciated. Although there is a voluminous literature on deafness, we have discovered that writings about deafness are scattered among differing idioms of scholarly discourse, conflicting ideological persuasions, and widely divergent methodologies.

In aiming for global understanding—the sense of the whole—the sociologist insists that there "is a category of ways of acting, thinking and feeling external to the individual, and endowed with a power of coercion by reason of which they control him" (Durkheim 1938, p. 3). Still, the sociologist appreciates biography and the ingenuity of the individual in adapting to and working with the social facts of his or her existence. A sociology of deafness will, then, proceed on three fronts simultaneously. It will attend to (1) the social facts of deafness, (2) the interrelatedness of these facts with larger societal matters, and (3) the place of the individual in this matrix of relationships.

The task envisioned in these chapters owes a debt to three developments in recent social-scientific research. The emergence of an ethnomethodological conception of social reality permits a full description of the deaf "natural attitude" and the "structure" of the experiences of deaf people.[1] The power of functionalism to move beyond the confines of patterned consciousness permits the demonstration of consequences within the structural processes, and advances in ethnographic-research techniques introduce precision and systematism to information about deafness.

The Ethnomethodological View of Social Reality

Largely as a reaction to the audacity of sociological versions of social reality,

1

a group of researchers working from a subjectivist tradition began to focus on everyday life. In particular, they emphasized that sociological theories often considered peoples' real experiences—and, more importantly, the ways in which people interpret and give meaning to their participtaion with others—as epiphenomenal, that is, as merely standing for and perhaps in relationship to the sociological reality. Thus conventional sociology, so the argument goes, looks through the world of common-sense knowledge. To the ethnomethodologist, this meant that sociology distorted the real world, portraying it as a product of rules or regularities without giving much concern to the nature of these rules, to how these rules become meaningful to individuals, or to how individuals apply them to concrete situations in the course of their everyday lives (Leiter 1980, p. 18).

In a series of frequently coordinated studies, ethnomethodological research has introduced a renewed appreciation of the subjective character of social reality. There are now several excellent reviews of the advances of this new strain of theory (Leiter 1980; Wallace and Wolf 1980; Turner 1978; Simmerman 1978; Morris 1977; and Mehan and Wood 1975). We draw on this rich literature for some insights essential to an understanding of the world of deafness.

First, people organize their experiences into complex, interrelated systems of knowledge.[2] These systems are common in that people apply them in practice to make sense out of what is going on in their immediate, everyday lives. These systems are the essential materials that make social life possible.

Second, social knowledge is *intersubjective*. It coheres by virtue of interpretations that persons make of each other. People act in accordance with their views following these interpretation procedures. The continuous "sense making" that people do together gives social reality a constructed character, that is, the quality of having been built from interaction.

Third, interaction creates reality, which manifests itself as multiple and layered phenomena. Some authors, such as Mehan and Wood (1975) have asserted that society consists of multiple social realities subject to radical change and dependent on systematic application in everyday life.

Fourth, discourse, both verbal and nonverbal, embodies social reality, This principle is usually discussed under the heading of *indexicality*, which, for our purposes, is taken to mean that modes of communication contain inferences to the contexts of their use and that the meanings of objects and events are inextricably bound in interactional contexts that consist of common-sense knowledge systems. To understand what has transpired, one must possess a description of the full context of the occasion.

We can draw many insights from this type of theorizing. For our purposes, however, these four are sufficient to show that social reality does exist, as Durkheim exhorted. But unlike Durkheim we believe that inquiry must appreciate the qualitative nature of that reality—its constructed, multiplicative, and malleable character. To describe the world of deafness as a social reality is a goal of this book.

Functionalism

Whereas the ethnomethodologist attends to the order of consciousness treating experience from the participant's point of view, traditional functional analysis has sought to move beyond what happens to people and how they see their experiences to posit appraisals about the state of society as a whole—a system of systems. Unfortunately, the development of functionalism as a school of thought has been flawed by problems of tautological error and reification. Further, largely because of changes in the politics of social science, the functionalists have been accused of a conservative bias and often bitterly attacked.[3] However, as Turner and Maryanski (1979, p. 140) attempt to show in their discussion of Parsons's work, "functional theory can provide investigators with common criteria for describing structures and processes in social systems." Once we have identified the dimensions of meaning in the world of deafness through the use of selected criteria, we can appreciate the holistic or systemic character of that world.

The crucial criteria that we employ are drawn from the writings of Weber, Parsons, and—in particular—Merton. These criteria are addressed to questions of structural interrelatedness or part-whole relationships (Turner and Maryanksi 1979, pp. 130-131). In order to assess the impact of interrelatedness among the various parts of the deaf world, we focus on observed consequences of policies, interchanges, and tendencies toward the construction and maintenance of patterned action. Our hypothesis is that the chief requisite in the world of the deaf is *adaptation*.[4] Other systemic problems must be understood as derivative from the processes of "seeking resources from the environment, converting them into usable facilities and then distributing them to the rest of the system" (Parsons, Bales, and Shils 1953).

With Merton (1963), we contend that the analysis of consequences of social action must be grounded in observation; investigation must focus on a particular structural pattern of interest, and attention should be given to the "net balance" of positive, negative, and neutral consequences of structure on the established requisites.

Hence, an analysis of the dimensions of deafness coupled with an appreciation of the symbolically originated and maintained character of the experiences must identify the reasons for the existence of the distinctive social reality. This type of explanatory endeavor, at least for people whose physical conditions give them a disadvantage in terms of full participation in the larger society, must attend to requisite features such as adaptive processes.

The patterns of consciousness found in everyday common-sense life provide the empirical documents for the assessments of consequences of part-whole relationships. The assessment of consequences goes beyond description and, therefore, is not limited to horizons of individually construed intersubjectivity. Still, consequences must be assessed in terms of their impact on everyday life, and the full appreciation of systemic operations depends on both a structural perspective and situationally restricted uses of adaptative strategies and processes.

The *functional criterion* informs two levels of involvement in the deaf world. At the structural level it addresses questions of interest and net balance, allowing for the assessments of a range of phenomena such as distorted communications, exploitation of selectively defined interest groups, and questions of solidarity within the deaf structures. At the psychological level, it addresses questions of what is distinctive about adaptive strategies and what profiles of social context relate to holistic requisites.

It has been argued openly (Davis 1959) that no clear distinction can be drawn between sociological and functional analysis. Today's analyst, with a dazzling variety of sociological imaginations to follow, may find this argument quaint. However, as Mills urged, questions of structure do entail "part-whole explanations" and the distinctions that Durkheim made between social and psychological realities; and the case for separate descriptions of their modalities still marks a *sociological* analysis.

Unfortunately, the subject of deafness came into focus at a time when the lens of the sociological camera was fractured, if not inoperative. The resultant findings about deafness thus appear to be many apparently unrelated snapshots. But by avoiding the polemics of higher theoretical sociology and by using insights from the literature in a consistent and convincing fashion, we may yet be able to put together the picture, or, at least, to frame the larger picture.

Ethnographic Data

Spradley (1979), writing about a quiet "ethnographic revolution," refers to the increased interest in and use of field observations and interviewing techniques designed to preserve in the description of cultural entities the "native's point of view." Whereas the ethnomethodologist who shares this concern for the participant's viewpoint stresses conceptualization of social interaction—perhaps at the expense of systematic description—the ethnoscientist looks to the systematic features of cultural systems of knowledge, perhaps at the expense of appreciating interactive phenomena.[5] The term *ethnographic* has come to stand for a way of doing research. The numbers of scholarly treatises and the range of topics and theories explored ethnographically would seem to support Spradley's contention that ethnographic research has come of age.

We have already outlined our concern for interactive perspectives. What we draw from ethnography pertains to three methodological issues. First, there are questions of the evidential status of such data; second, the notion of systematism; and third, the question of representation or generality. Each issue can be briefly discussed within the context of a sociology of deafness.

The literature on deafness contains two kinds of studies that account for virtually all the information available. Experimental or quasi-experimental designs characterize many of the psychological and psycholinguistic studies, both cross-sectional and longitudinal. Examples include Furth's (1964, 1973) work on cognition; Moores's (1978) evaluations of pedadogical techniques; surveys of attitudes; and demographic or socioeconomic profiles that claim to define variables and their relationships. All these efforts direct the researcher to a "cause-and-effect" imagery. We do not mean to criticize this often excellent literature and its emphasis on testing hypotheses that pertain to deaf people's thinking, emotions, and behavior. We wish only to suggest that such research does not necessarily require fidelity to distinctions, contrasts, or actions among members of a deaf culture.

To the extent that one's purposes for inquiry do require such fidelity, the aforementioned literature may have little or no relevance. In fact, ethnomethodologists' forte seems to be showing the separate yet interdependent lines of reasoning involved in "scientific versions" of reality, on the one hand, and common-sense life worlds on the other. To this end, ethnographic accounts of deafness must describe the culture even to the extent that that culture is influenced by a "scientific" version of it.

It is useless to attempt to divide information into "hard" and "soft." An experimentally evaluated hypothesis is not "harder," and thus more informative, than is a systematic analysis of descriptive information. The ethnographic approach merely aims for a different end—the understanding of organized, culturally circumscribed experiences. This does not make it a "softer" approach, nor is the information less reliable simply because it is not expressed quantitatively. In fact, Cicourel (1974c), in his replication of a study of Jamaican fertility in Argentina, demonstrates that "hard facts" often mask a use of common-sense knowledge.

> The researcher's use of particulars he selectively labels "data" is part of a broader activity whereby he sustains an everyday existence within which the researcher proceeds and on which he trades implicitly. Every description of scientific activity relies on this existence even though the researcher does not acknowledge that he must sustain this common sense world in connection with his claims to knowledge about an environment of objects that relies on implicit, culturally organized verbal and nonverbal conditions. [pp.:113-114]

It is sufficient for our purposes to recognize at once that studies of

"culturally organized verbal and nonverbal conditions" require methods appropriate to the task. To be sure, ethnography does create a social reality through
the process of following rules for the proper conduct of the research (Leiter
1980, p. 89). However, the relationship between the creation of an ethnography
and the world of everyday life can either become the subject of a second related inquiry, on the one hand, or, on the other, be rendered public through
the explicit description of the relationship itself.

The information presented in this book is ethnographically informed and
presented. It is not exploratory in the sense of awaiting "better" data for fuller
testing. Nor is it less valid simply because it follows different methodological
criteria from those used in most literature on deafness. Rather, its validity
must be judged according to how well it preserves the participant's standpoint;
whether it can generate systematically distinctions and meanings recognizable
by members of the deaf culture themselves in degree and proportion to their
knowledge; whether it informs the outsider of this insider perspective; and
whether it makes explicit the methods of presentation by which these ends
are said to have been achieved.

The second type of study that dominates the literature is the single-
informant, linguistic study (Stokoe and Kuschel 1979). Much of the material
and many of the ideas presented in this book are predicated on studies of this
type. Information about language as a rule-governed system best comes from
those most adept in the use of the rules. Thus the linguist seeks out the "best
signers," the articulate, and the bright to serve as informants. The wisdom
of this tactic is apparent in the spectacular results of recent studies. The list of
contributors starts with Stokoe and grows to include Woodward, Battison,
Markowicz, Wilbur, Klima, Bellugi and others. Our knowledge of American
Sign Language (ASL) in particular and of signing systems in general has grown
enormously.

However, these linguistic studies have also created a reality, an abstract
system of rules and elements not necessarily isomorphic to native experience.
And, as many field researchers will attest, the informant one starts with may
not be the one with which one finishes. He or she will also learn well, and soon
the informant may takes on the attitude of a researcher. Worse, in the study of
languages the informant may become a new "school grammarian," proscribing
and prescribing the use of the language.

Douglas (1976) writes of typical uses of informants in social-science research. He identifies several possibly false assumptions that underlie the relationship between researcher and informant. The first of these is the assumption
of the homogeneity of the phenomenon being studied (Douglas 1976, pp. 45ff).
In connection with ASL, the diversity or variants of sign are understood as
degrees and dimensions of departure from the central rule system, not as conflicting forms. Second, researchers assume that, through cooperation with their
sources of information the most-reliable "data" possible can be obtained.

Consequently, an aversion to any kind of antagonism between researcher and informant is built into the research act. The researcher becomes very willing to accommodate the demands and idiosyncrasies of the informant; and, as Douglas suggests, the informant may become more than willing to tell the researcher what he or she is looking for. Researcher and informant, in effect, team up to produce an interpretation of the phenomenon being studied. The relationship that this version bears to everyday life is seldom treated explicitly.

In the research described in this book, however, we have tried not to avoid conflict, and to challenge informants, matching them one against the other—sometimes literally, most of the time imaginatively through the use of various analytic devices. We have questioned the homogeneity of the deaf culture, and we have tried not to assume that confidence and truth are synonyms.

Nevertheless, we work with ethnographic techniques because we do want to posit degrees of systematism. We aim to unveil rules, domains, attributes, and semantic relationships. When we exhibit a taxonomy or demonstrate a componential contrast, we know full well that this is a created reality. The germane question is whether this version of the reality moves us toward a sociological understanding.

Critics often raise questions of the representativeness of the data collected through ethnographic research. They attempt to apply a logic of sampling distributions to ethnographic materials. Sturtevant writes that ethnoscientific accounts can be thought of as "the system of knowledge and cognition typical of a given culture," and that a "culture amounts to the sum of a given society's folk classifications, all of that society's ethnoscience, its particular ways of classifying its materials and social universe" (Sturtevant 1964, p. 100). Although it is obvious that no single person knows all the knowledge systems implicit within the full range of their social participation, it is even less perspicacious to expect a random sample to reveal anything other than fragments of those systems. Spradley (1979, p. 46) advises that a persistent problem in ethnographic research is the "failure to locate a good informant," by which he means an informant "who can assist the novice [any] ethnographer in learning about that informant's culture while at the same time learning the interviewing skills." He continues to enumerate minimal requirements for selecting an informant. For our purposes, these amount to postponing the selection of informants until after an acculturation period. This means that in working with the deaf, it may be necessary to learn generally before understanding specific interviews or observations. Several different informants may be used, and switching among them may be quite appropriate. The ethnographer of the deaf must be careful not to be misled by ignorance about the informant's place within the world of deafness. Such ignorance can result in failure to recognize the multiple-layered, interdependent nature of interactional meanings among the deaf. A lifelong educator, either deaf or hearing, may serve well as an informant for that dimension of the total system but may be an unreliable source about aspects of the structure such as the perceptions deaf people have of the hearing. Likewise, a deaf informant may know little about hearing parents. Although we want to stress the roles that perceptions—even stereotypes—play in interaction among, say, hearing parents and deaf people, we also want to separate the types of perceptions and the knowledge systems that generate them.

We employed a variety of informants in the preparation of the various chapters in this book. We believe that we "sampled" at least the major facets of the culture of deaf, where we take that culture to be inclusive of the hearing people serving in ancillary roles. These chapters do not make up a sociology of the deaf. They are more like forays into a new and different world, designed to bring back information to be used in constructing an interpretation of that world. In this sense, the papers are ethnographically informed and are representative of the multiple dimensions of deafness.

The Dimensions of the World of Deafness

The deaf culture is heterogeneous. It cannot be treated as though it evolved independently from the dominant culture that serves as its host. It is a fragmented culture, almost out of place in the modern world. It resembles the cultures of other oppressed people, but it is also unique in some respects. We will focus on six dimensions of the meanings of deafness.

1. The linguistic dimensions are probably the most visible and easily documented. To be sure, the complete grammar of American Sign Language has yet to be written. Still, sufficient information exists to permit us to sketch the linguistic environment of deafness. In chapter 2 we will stress the dominance of spoken English, the distinctiveness of American Sign Language, and the unique interactions between these two domains.

2. The peculiar social character of deafness as a handicap results in inordinate importance being placed on educational institutions by the hearing administrators and researchers who formulate policy; by hearing parents, whose lives are affected by these policies; by deaf children themselves, whose socialization experiences are directly influenced; and, finally, by adults whose heritage as deaf people often derives from an educational institution and who themselves may also be parents of deaf children. In chapter 3 we will explicate the images of social interaction underlying policies and point to consequences of the policies.

3. Questions of class and class consciousness have rarely been addressed in either speculative of empirical reasearch. This is due to a lack of any conceptual framework that could show the relevance of obvious class patterns in the consciousness of the deaf themselves as well as that of ancillary hearing people. These patterns are relative to those that exist in the larger society. In chapter 4

we will develop this relevance through a description of a contrast between "natural attitudes" of hearing middle- and lower-class persons and members of the deaf community.

4. Most people who are deaf have hearing parents. Hence, insofar as early socialization experiences are concerned, these parents play an important role in creating the environments within which children acquire interactional competencies. We devote chapter 5 to depicting the components of these environments and analyzing the way in which they become part of the complex matrix of social interaction that makes up the homes of deaf children.

5. The deaf, like other groups with distinctive social identities, have created their own ways of making sense of everyday life. They have a community. Although a full description of this community is beyond the scope of this book, in chapter 6 we have focused on how this community imparts predefined conceptions of types of hearing people and what functions these conceptions have in cross-modal communicative exchanges.

6. We cast the broadest net possible to portray the multifaceted structure of deafness. In chapter 7 we examine the survival adaptations employed by deaf people and treat them as negotiated outcomes of framed meanings that are ready made and given by society. Our analysis leads to a discussion of the phenomenon of marginality, which is manifested uniquely in the lives of the deaf.

Finally, in chapter 8 we explore the impact of modern life on the cultural and social reality of deafness. If, as we suggest, the adaptations deaf people make are "framed" by larger societal structures, then, as those structures change in form and function, the character of the deaf experience is affected. Questions of the direction and consequences of these changes are entertained.

Notes

1. A *natural attitude* refers to phenomenologically informed information about the state of wide-awake attention that is typical of persons in their routine pursuits of daily affairs. The natural attitude is "the basis of [a person's] interpretation of the life world as a whole and in its various aspects. The life world is the world of the natural attitude. In it, things are taken for granted" (Wagner 1970, p. 320).

2. In this sense, ethnomethodology focuses on "common sense." As a perspective, however, it regards all potential and actual knowledge systems equally practical in everyday life. Therefore, even the scientist lives in the world of common sense; and, although he or she may act on the basis of a "finding," this knowledge does not differ qualitatively from, say, superstition or religious maxims (see Mehan and Wood 1975, pp. 8-33).

3. Functional thought, although never really lost in sociological

explanation, did go underground during the 1960s and early 1970s. The reasons for this loss of vogue have been detailed by Turner, Gouldner, and others. Fortunately for our purposes, recent literature has reintroduced some important issues that functionalism attempted to address. This literature seeks to give functional thought its place in the general efforts of constructing sociological explanations (Turner 1978; Turner and Maryanski 1979; Moore 1978).

4. In modern functional theory, especially that influenced by the writings of Parsons, attempts are made to identify explicitly universal problems of action systems. Although any social system must attend to a full range of "problems," from goal attainment and adaptation to integration and pattern maintenance, systems do vary both in emphasis on problems and in the importance that problems possess for that total system (Parsons 1951; Turner and Maryanski 1979).

5. There are several excellent articles that compare ethnomethodological and ethnoscientific approaches (Psathas 1968; Leiter 1980). Generally, we hold that these "research attitudes" can complement one another, especially when attention is given to interactive phenomena among cultural knowledge systems. Ethnographic literature ranges over a wide variety of styles of scholarship. Sturtevant, Goodenough, and a host of others have done elaborate methodological descriptions of exotic, nonmodern cultures. Spradley (1971) has employed ethnographic techniques to analyze cultural domains in urban society such as those of tramps, for example, or even that of a family with a deaf child. For our purposes we take ethnography to denote an "emic" standpoint in descriptions, coupled with some systematic devices for classification of this standpoint.

2
The Linguistic Environment: Its Sociological Significance

Although deafness inhibits the normal acquisition of spoken language, it does not follow that deaf people live in a simplified, underdeveloped linguistic environment. The language world of the deaf is rich and complex. A description of that world is a requirement of the sociology of deafness, since the meanings of the everyday lives of deaf people are played out through the various aspects of language.

Deaf people live in a world that comprises two separate but interdependent languages: English as they comprehend and use it, and the American Sign Language (ASL). These two languages may be described as distinct domains, each with its own form and function. In practical life, each can be performed in such a manner that the form of the one does not beguile the other.

English and American Sign Language coexist in the organization of deaf experiences and meanings. In a sense, ASL is a minority language that shows subtly in its development and operation the dominance of English (see Battison 1978). Still, signs resist the influences of spoken grammars. Deaf people are exposed to languages in conflict, and this has resulted in varieties of both languages as vernaculars.[1] These varieties we identify as *signed/written English, written deaf English,* and *pidgin signs.* Although not of equal importance to an indexing of meanings, each may be placed within the total structure of the linguistics of deafness. In order to understand the significance of the varieties, we must discuss the two salient features of the environment.

The American Sign Language Domain

> The typifying medium par excellence by which socially derived knowledge is transmitted is the vocabulary of everyday language. The vernacular of everyday life is primarily a language of named things and events, and any name includes a typification and generalization referring to the relevance system prevailing in the linguistic in-group which found the named thing significant enough to provide a separate term for it . . . vernacular can be interpreted as a treasure house of ready made pre-constituted types and characteristics. [Schutz 1962, p. 14]

The handicap that closes natural access to the ordinary world of vernaculars produces its own complex linguistic form. Within this form the meanings of everyday life are embodied for the deaf person. Cicourel and Boese (1972) show that the social reality of the deaf child whose socialization occurs within a context of signs differs from that of either the hearing child or the deaf child with hearing parents. When we include that large group of deaf people who having grown old without any "native" language and who later take on ASL as their true language, we are in a position to suggest that the social reality of deafness is indexed by signs.

Analysis may assume two directions from the principle of *embodied meanings*.[2] The first is to show that the sign-language community is structurally similar to other communities. For example, the concept of *cherology* introduced by Stokoe (1978, pp. 29-54) convinces us that, although signs have unique aspects, they are like words in that they can be analyzed in terms of both their *phonology* and their *morphology*. The second, as suggested by Peng (1977), is to explore how unique aspects reflect themselves in social structures. Hence, we can ask to what degree an aspect like *simultaneity* (Peng 1977, p. 28)—that is, being able to sign two cheremic features at the same time (one on each hand, or one on the hand and the other on the face, for instance)—affects the interpersonal dynamics of, say, the organization of conversation.

Since the thrust of this book is to move toward theorizing about deafness, we must focus on how variants of linguistic usages transform into principles of organization. Expressed in Schutz's terms, we are interested in the question of how the particulars of a vernacular relate to "systems of relevance"; that is, what is important for the tasks at hand, given the cultural categories available?[3] We will develop the argument that such systems of relevance are primarily adaptive processes.

We understand that social reality is constructed (Schutz 1962, p. 52) within a boundary of "we-relations." The common-sense thinking of people living daily among their fellows connects them in outward relations of interaction. With these theoretical remarks in mind, we can offer several sensitizing observations about the domain of signs and its relevance for a sociology of deafness.

The principle of embodiment—that everyday discourse indexes social reality—holds that American Sign Language, as a vernacular, contains the meanings of deafness. These meanings are tacit, consisting of what Garfinkel (1967) has called "backgrounded expectancies." The meanings, in turn, comprise categories of common-sense knowledge that may be discussed at the levels of lexicon, syntax, and semantics. Lexically, we can collect terms that reflect the world view of the deaf. Syntactically, we can identify rules for the use of the terms. Finally, semantically, we can demonstrate the pragmatics of both lexicon and syntax.

If signs embody the meanings of deafness, then the limits and interactive contacts of the domain constitute the boundaries of the community. Mead's (1934) concept of the "generalized other" and its relationship to the self suggests this constitutive arrangement. With respect to the emergence of the self, the assumption must be made that symbols mean the same to all those who use them (the linguistic in-group). Mead (1934) referred to this state as the *universality of symbols*. For practical purposes, this means that a symbol (category) is universal when users of it impute similar meanings to situations of interaction in which the symbol is said to apply; in other words, they use it in the same way. Speakers (signers) assume that they know the mind of the other and, by an act of imagination, place themselves in relationship to others. To the extent that persons "take on the role of the others," common meanings emerge and the bases for social organization are formed. An image of oneself arises, then, whenever the individual has the ability to take on the attitude of the other as if it were his own and then to act on the basis of this intersubjective understanding. Thus a person acts "in-order-to" take a place in a community (see Pfuetze 1954, p. 78; Hewitt 1976, pp. 92-104).

It follows that signs, the language or medium through which symbolic communication occurs, define the boundary between the deaf and hearing communities and function to structure the deaf community itself. In subsequent chapters we shall show how the process of defining the "generalized other" bears directly on the quality of cross-modal communicative exchanges.

As a language, ASL has unique properties (Stokoe 1978; Peng 1977). Although it does clearly qualify as a "natural language" (it has an "atomic" structure; it is rule governed; and its rule system seems capable of indefinitely elaborate performances) the structure of signs seems adapted to the constraints of visual perceptions (Siple 1978). This means that the elemental features of the language, cheremes and syntax, conform to "sharp contrasts" of the eye rather than to those of the ear. Several researchers have described these elements (Baker and Padden 1978; Klima and Bellugi 1979; Wilbur 1979). What is significant here is the recognition that a unique medium for communication may mean, in fact, unique communications. A sociological conception of the language of the deaf must attend to questions of (1) the extent to which linguistic particularities condition the quality of social processes, and (2) the practical motivational systems that may be embedded within a "vocabulary of signs."

The English or Hearing Domain

Spoken English is, even if mastered with "native-like" competency by a deaf person, a language of hearing. For the deaf person it is a language that must be learned. It is not acquired naturally (Cicourel and Boese 1972), and its use requires the introduction of some substitution for the self-monitoring loop—hearing oneself talk—taken for granted by hearing speakers.

From the point of view of the deaf, speaking is hearing. The boundaries between the deaf and the hearing are, thus, maintained by attitudes toward

English. A deaf person does not have to be competent in English in order to engage in this categorization. It is knowledge about—not of—English that is the salient consideration. Therefore, we can conclude that English constitutes the hearing world from the vantage point of deafness.

The use of English by a deaf person requires a cognitive effort not only to produce intelligible utterances but also to reconcile an essentially unsuccessful movement from a familiar symbolic universe to an alien one. The concept of *alternation* can help us to grasp the social significance of movement from one language world to another. According to Berger and Luckmann (1967, p. 157), an alternation experience is a total shift that can occur in the ways available to an individual for interpreting the meaning of life. When such experiences happen, persons acquire new, ready-made identities—symbolically, they are reborn. Radical shifts in realities are typically eased through a *plausibility structure* that functions to guide an individual from the first to the second symbolic universe. Such structures are composed of statuses and are peopled by significant others.

To the degree that a deaf person must use English and since the nuances of implication that English carries are beyond the reach of the "non-native" speaker, the switch to English is never a complete alternation. The deaf person carries a plausibility structure of his or her own into any communicative exchange, and thus the use of English for the deaf is incomplete in a sociological sense. How the deaf know the hearing—their definitions of the hearing "other"—will be, likewise, incomplete and influenced by truncated knowledge.

The consequences of these forced and incomplete alternation experiences are of immense importance since the conceptions that the deaf have of the hearing and the quality of deaf-deaf as well as deaf-hearing relations are influenced by a context of conceptions of self, other, and community.

Even a cursory observation of the lives of deaf people reveals that a great deal of "negotiation" goes on among these conceptions. This is reflected in what sociolinguists call *code switching* (Fishman 1972). With changing situations of interaction and with corresponding acts in order to achieve some end, the deaf person will consciously select the most-appropriate medium of discourse. In the intimacy of community, signs give interaction an intimate (in-group) quality. When a deaf person is in the presence of real or anticipated symbols of the hearing domain, shifts of medium generally in the direction of English can be detected. Depending on the adaptations affected and the pressures from the "frames" of societal interaction (Goffman 1974), the deaf person will tend to see English in perfunctory terms: speaking is pro forma of life among the hearing. English has a quality, in Parsons's (1951, pp. 80-88) terms, of specificity. It is a medium of exchange for the purposes of "instrumental practicality." Had Toennies studied the deaf, he might have suggested that the channel through which the deaf attempt to play out the requirements of *gesellschaft* is English. Of course, no full community or *gemeinschaft* can be constructed by means of such artificiality.

It is in the written variant of English that the properties of exchange as "rational" are best exemplified. Only when the constraints of modern society are their strongest do we see the deaf use written English. They use it out of ritualistic necessity. A conspicuous use of alien English forms illustrates an adaptation through which a person attempts to gain acceptance and assimilation into a hearing world.

We know that, as a group, the deaf are nearly illiterate (Moores 1978). This means that as a people the deaf are impeded in full participation in society not only in orally defined opportunities but also in the *written* institutions of society which, prima facie, remain open to them. This point has been widely made in the literature on deafness (Moores 1978; Furth 1973). However, the point is usually made as part of a suggestion that the deaf are misunderstood by ill-informed hearing people. Of equal significance is the observation that written language generally changes at a much slower rate than spoken and that written language embodies the traditions of a culture in a much more status-bound manner than the oral media (Goody and Watt 1972). Thus the deaf must deal with a twice-removed language form (once from ASL, once from spoken English). Further, they must enact traditions that are not only alien to them but also perhaps old fashioned, at least in comparison with more-vernacular forms. The deaf person perforce interactions within a medium that embodies most clearly a communicative organization that has changed slowly and that requires not only oral mastery of English grammar but also supplemental and status-laden competencies. To the extent that the community of the deaf is *gemeinschaftlich*, its linguistic form is "oral" in the sense of a tribal, nonliterate medium (see Curtis 1978). Written English is a linear form that is much more "conventional" than signs. For the deaf, then, the proper use of written English involves much more than learning the rudiments of reading and writing.

Often, among themselves and within the constraints of, for instance, a TTY conversation (TTYs are teletypewriter adaptors that allow the deaf to use the telephone among themselves), the deaf will write in what has been called *written deaf English*. They borrow, as it were, from the lexicon of English and match it to the syntax of their signs. The result is a "new form," which is written and which, in some cases, cannot be understood without knowledge of the grammar of signs. When the deaf write to the hearing, they try to move toward standard English. Their sentences may even manifest "hypercorrective" phenomena (Labov 1972).

For instance, a deaf person might write the sentence, "I town zoom yesterday." This would be a English sentence according to a sign grammar. It could be translated, "Yesterday I rushed into town." Sign grammar requires an ordering by sequence, concreteness, and a sense of time. This sentence conforms to these requirements, since it lists the sequence (place toward which the action is oriented), has the concrete object near the beginning of the sentence, and employs a sign tense marker, "yesterday," indicating past tense.

When the deaf write to the hearing or whenever they perceive the symbols of the hearing domain to be pertinent to a particular communicative exchange, they attempt to do less structuring of English words with the sign grammar and more of what they regard as correct English. They might, then, write a sentence like, "I must know if Lucy have happen lost or hurt."[4] This sentence is significant because it illustrates hypercorrection and can be unequivocally understood only according to a sign or written-sign gr. nmar.

The "if, then" English construction d/es not exist in signs. A transliteration of the sentence would be, "I must know Lucy lost hurt, which, finish," or, in standard English, "I must know if Lucy has been lost or hurt." The original sentence is hypercorrective because the "if" construction was introduced under "official" circumstances (in communication with a legal counsel in connection with an important trial). The "if" seemed to the deaf man who wrote it to be an English-sentence unit appropriate to the formal circumstances of the communication. Nevertheless, he used it as if it were the sign "which."

Such sentences in general and this one in particular have the "deep structures" of sign grammar but illustrate the influence on language expressions of knowledge about English interpreted through a status hierarchy. As English, the sentence is ambiguous because the verb-elaboration and clause-supporting elements embody several meanings. The construction of the clause could mean, "Is it going to happen?" or "Will it happen?" or "Has it already happened?" or "Is it now happening?"

However, if the sentence is seen as using rules of sign grammar, then its meaning is unambiguous. The deep structure can be described as follows: a noun phrase consisting of two modifying elements telling about the state of the object of the phrase, the pronoun (I, must know). The verb phrase consists of a verb construction telling about the action and marking time (tense). This is accomplished through the use of a conditional coupled with a "finish" occurrence (have happen). Woodward (1973) has identified this use of "finish" as a allomorph of perfective aspect and as a characteristic of pidgin sign. A final noun phrase consists of a noun and optional modifiers:

[(if, have happen) . . . (Lucy, lost hurt which) . . . (finish)]

Pidginization Processes

The processes of pidginization has been widely documented. As Trudgill (1974, p. 167) puts it, a "pidgin language is a lingua franca which has no native speakers." It results from contact among several languages where there is a dominant language. It consists of a borrowing among the languages, generally with a simplification of grammar and a reduction of lexicon and syntax. As Trudgill points out, however, this is not always the case; a pidgin may become quite sophisticated. Pidgins are, as forms, capable of the expression of complicated meanings (see Fromkin and Rodman 1978, pp. 268-270; Hall 1955). The particular character of a pidgin will vary with the sociological context of its use.

Woodward (1973) and others (Wilbur 1979) have suggested that there is a pidgin sign. In fact, this pidgin is often the signed counterpart of, and the basis for, written deaf English. According to Woodward (1973), the syntax of pidgin sign can be described. He cites six features that mark a pidginization of signs: first, the variable use of articles; second, reduplication for noun plurals; third, the selective use of "invented" signs for the English copula; fourth, the use of both the English progressive aspect (be + verb + ing: is going); fifth, the use of reduplication to reduce structure; and sixth, the use of an allomorph "finish" following the verb to show perfective aspect and the truncated use of incorporations (see Woodward 1973; Wilbur 1979; Reilly and McIntire 1980).

We may conclude that (1) pidginization results from a clash of linguistic domains, (2) the dominance of English is reflected in the pidgin, and (3) the pidgin serves a function of mediation between signs and English by allowing sign to exist as a separate domain while contacting hearing signers. This is the sense in which Trudgill refers to a pidgin language as a lingua franca.[5]

Sign English is another variant within the language environment of deafness. It is a transliterating device, and its distinguishing characteristic is an effort to render English visual through the borrowing of an invention of signs to correspond to the English "parts of speech." This means, of course, that little regard is given to the function that signs played within the sign grammar. We mention this here to stress that the pidgin does embody elements of the signs.

A sketch of the linguistic environment of deafness is offered in figure 2-1. The two domains are partially independent. In the contact and influence of one on the other the following patterns apply:

1. Signs influence pidgin signs, and both signs and pidgin influence written deaf English, although the influences on written deaf English are disproportionally English.
2. The contact of signs and English produces a pidgin.
3. English influences sign English and the pidgin.
4. The pidgin insulates signs from direct influence by the dominant English language of the larger society.
5. Written and sign English, as well as speech, function primarily in an instrumental capacity for deaf people.
6. Signs and English embody distinctive vernaculars for the deaf and the hearing as well as for what the deaf think about the hearing.

The overall environment may be described as *diglossic* (Stokoe 1970).[6] Signs and English for the deaf stand in particular standardized forms where

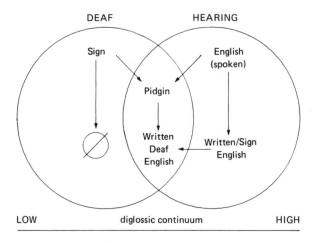

Figure 2-1. The Linguistic Environment of the Deaf

English as a distinct variety of the total environment exists side by side with signs. These juxtaposed forms are widely distributed throughout the language community. And, as is generally the case, the term *diglossic* defines a high and a low variety—English and signs, respectively.

We have depicted a complex and interdependent set of relationships that constitute the linguistic environment of deafness. We contend that these domains are properly conceived as vernaculars in conflict. The native deaf signer, unfettered by the influences of English, is an artifact of a linguistic methodology. We suggest that instead of focusing on the pure formal properties of either ASL or English, we look at the everyday common-sense world of deafness in which both domains interact. There we see the foundations for the realities of deafness.

Notes

1. We take vernaculars to be performances of a language that are carried out within the context of everyday life. After Fishman (1970) and Steward (1968), we stress that vernaculars are defined largely as matters of attitudes toward language. Chiefly, this means that vernaculars are not necessarily standard in their usages within a speech community. By focusing on performances, we expect to be able to uncover speakers' or signers' "procedures for doing activities," permitting us "both to replicate our original data and to generate new instances that fellow members will find recognizable" (Turner 1970, p. 187).

2. The term *embodiment* has several distinct usages in phenomenological and existential literature. It can refer to the interpretive competence acquired by a person to understand "place" in the world—that is, who the person is and what his or her surroundings mean. In this sense, we often see phrases such as the "embodied self." It can also refer to the general notion that meaning is discoverable within a phenomenon itself. Hence, language "embodies" the meanings of everyday life—that is, the sense of being in society is rendered concrete by expression in perceptible forms (see O'Neil 1973; Zaner and Ihde 1973; Cicourel 1974a).

3. Weigert (1975) has explicated a "theory of motivation" from the writings of Schutz. This "theory" places emphasis on interactional situations in which persons impute a perceived "time" dimension and a reciprocal quality of knowing. For the present analytic intent, we note that this theory makes us sensitive to what deaf people think they know about hearing people and themselves as well as to the means through which they arrive at these "in-order-to" and "because" types of known and imputed motives (Weigert 1975, p. 85).

4. This sentence, like many others used throughout this book, is taken from field notes and is an actual sentence used by a deaf person in a situation of everyday life. This particular sentence was an important piece of information in a legal case. It was written by a deaf man in an attempt to communicate with a hearing, nonsigning social worker.

5. Trudgill writes that "a pidgin language . . . is derived from a 'normal' language through simplification: most often reduction in vocabulary and grammar, and elimination of complexities and irregularities. There is also usually a certain admixture, often considerable, from the native language or languages of those who use it" (1974, p. 167).

6. No definitive study is available either of the pidginization process or of the exact nature of the diglossic relationship between ASL and English. However, Stokoe (1978) and Reilly and McIntire (1980) have suggested that both phenomena have unique features. Pidgin sign English (PSE) can be ranked on the rule-governed use of facial expressions, showing that movement toward the ASL end of the continuum implies more use of the face in a language-like way. Likewise, diglossia is complicated by rapidly changing evaluations of ASL by its new and old users and by amorphously formed societal positions toward it. Reilly and McIntire depict the continuum as follows:

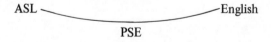

ASL ——————————————————— English

PSE

They note that PSE enjoys lower status than ASL among the deaf and lower status than English among the hearing. Here we focus on the interaction of domains as conceived by the deaf. Pidgin falls within an overlap (it embodies

meanings both from deafness and from hearing structures). Therefore, "attitudes" must entail reciprocal evaluations (of the deaf as they view the hearing
world). Stokoe's early characterization of PSE as having a status higher than
ASL but lower than spoken English seems closer to the intent of this analysis.
We must add that we are not talking about an empirical problem since data of
interactive phenomena are fundamentally unavailable through merely asking a
person. Our depiction treats domains as interactive and theoretically suggests a
hierarchical arrangement, given the "natural attitude" of the deaf, especially
with regard to their understanding of the hearing world. The fact that deaf
people prefer signing ASL over PSE and that they may even disdain "English"
does not alter societally distributed evaluations of ASL. According to Fishman
(1972) societies may well be and often are bilingual in the sense of having a
large portion of people able to use two languages, but society still may be
disglossic in terms of preferred language—that is, the societal organization of
discourse. In such situations groups of people may well prefer and regard as
superior a "minority language." Diglossia is a feature of societal reality.

3 Ordinary Knowledge and the Meanings of Deafness

Research findings showing that sign language may be learned among deaf children in ways consistent with the learning of oral languages for hearing children are now quite familiar (Klima and Bellugi 1979; Meadow 1980; Schlesinger and Meadow 1972). It is also widely recognized that these findings are often used to promote one educational policy over another. (Moores 1978; Markowicz 1972). Some researchers erroneously believe that once the most-valid conclusions possible have been formulated, policymakers will evaluate existing practices in terms of the current state of knowledge. These "scientists" presume that research findings are cumulative, leading us toward ever more-complete approximations of the truth. To them, it is simply a matter of time and properly conducted research before the "best" groundwork for educational policy becomes available.

However, ethnomethodologists like Cicourel (1974c) have taken great pains to show that "expert" knowledge of findings is itself interpreted according to a variety of considerations that are not strictly covered by methodological rigor. Further, the impact on educational policy of what is known about deafness is far from direct. Instead, a "finding" is filtered through a complex and layered structure of common-sense cultural knowledge, each layer resulting in a possible new interpretation.

A policy, then, is a consequence of the way in which people negotiate, from often distinct stances, a mutually tolerable version of the consequences of a course of action. One way to think about the process of how policies operate in practice is to observe that programs drawn from research always rest on a view of what is "ordinary" within a larger cultural context. For example, to suggest that sign language *can* be acquired naturally and spontaneously and therefore *should* be so acquired rests on a series of assumptions that deafness be thought of in a particular way by hearing persons who are in intimate contact with the deaf (see Sudnow 1965; Garfinkel 1967). This means that whenever attention is drawn to a person because of an unusual behavior, one may make sense out of the extraordinary by regarding it as an instance of what everybody knows—that is, by using typical understandings available generally in culture. When proposing that education of the deaf should use

This chapter is a revised version of Jeffrey E. Nash, "Some Sociolinguistic Aspects of Deaf Education Policy," *Sociological Focus* (October 1976): 349-360. Used with permission.

communication systems that will produce results as measured by scholastic or vocational achievement, the role of the common-sense, taken-for-granted everyday world of cultural knowledge may be overlooked.

One of the reasons that the use of visual forms of communication and particularly the native language of the deaf (American Sign Language, or ASL) is restricted—often in very subtle ways (see Erting 1980)—in the education of young deaf children is that, by implication, these approaches question what is given as "ordinary" knowledge and its function, namely, to account for the problematic nature of deafness for hearing people. The "total-communication" approach (signs and speech used simultaneously) makes the assumption that all forms of language competency are equally socially acceptable. In fact, it is interesting to note that a major thrust of the research on total communication has been to show that signing does not interfere with the effort to speak (Schlesinger and Meadow 1972; Benderly 1980). Either to advocate one educational approach over another or to consider all to be equally important involves hidden cultural agenda for thinking about deafness.

A detailed consideration of what some of these tacit agenda are follows two routes. On the one hand, policies coming from research on language learning make assumptions about deaf people themselves. These assumptions involve either deliberate or incidental interpretations of deaf people as a subtype of people in general, people who have a different manifestation of linguistic competence. The subtype is then regarded as having characteristics that either may relieve certain obligations in "normal" social contact or may suggest domains independent of and not necessarily implicated by ordinary interaction. For instance, hands about the face and the use of exaggerated facial and body gestures, all of which are ordinarily unacceptable for hearing persons, are reinterpreted as part of normal conversation or "how deaf people talk." In this alternative context there is a general acceptance of the role of hands, which means, among other things, a renegotiation of ordinary meanings for the use of hands in communication. Another way to think of this is to realize that, for hearing people, gestures are ordinarily regarded as *expressive* only. Judgments about deaf people within this context rest on the belief that contact between hearing and deaf people will result in both types of people imputing these same characteristics to each other—a kind of cultural pluralism in everyday life.

On the other hand, assumptions about the primacy of spoken English tend to deny any necessity to think of deaf people as extraordinary. In fact, a working maxim of this "oralist" or "ordinary" policy is that deaf people, especially small children not yet exposed to sign language, are simply people who cannot hear. These children and perhaps some deaf adults may be "successful," with appropriate amounts of work, in the sense that they become just like anyone else. This position is predicted on a belief that people will impute hearing-like characteristics to deaf people—that is, accept the speech of the deaf as coming from something like "hearing" others' speech and accept talking as the universal medium of social interaction. One must keep in mind that these assumptions may, to varying degrees, be based on educational techniques other than speech training and lip reading, such as Signing Exact English and Cued Speech.

Interchangeability and the Clash of Persons

A sociolinguistic perspective suggests that assumptions such as those discussed here, appropriate to different situations, are the basis for all social interaction. This perspective holds that most social contacts involve an element of mutual interpretation. Several researchers (see Leiter 1980) have offered concepts intended to make the content of an interpretation easier to discover. One such concept, that of the *reciprocity of perspectives*, refers to the assumptions people make in various kinds of social interaction such that each person imagines the other's standpoint, with both persons taking it for granted that the other's viewpoint is identical—reciprocal, for practical purposes. This assumption becomes an ideal suggesting that both would have the same experiences if they were to change places. This ideal goes unchallenged until one party questions it (the problem of counterevidence).

    Oralism is committed to establishing a version of this interchangeability that maintains that deaf people, with proper work, can in fact "see" things as hearing persons do. In other words, the deaf can have identical understandings with the hearing only if they are capable of speaking English.

    We know, however, that mutual understanding is not a matter of mere linguistic equivalence. Obviously, it is not necessary for persons to talk to each other with the same words in order to understand each other. A condition of human communicative systems is the necessity to be able to form an image of the other's intention and motivation, not simply to use elements according to a rule or fixed pattern. There are many possible motivations for and realizations of modes of communication; these, of course, often vary for two people in conversation. If we examine carefully the context within which the assumptions of oralists operate, we see that oralism does often become a basis for interpreting deafness for the hearing who need to account for deafness in a way that shores up threatened cultural knowledge systems. This applies most clearly, of course, to hearing parents of deaf children.

    Certainly not all parents are avowed oralists; however, the backgrounds of hearing parents are often consistent with the oralist policy. That policy comprises characteristics necessary to establish an understanding that then can become the grounding for deciding what it means to have a deaf offspring. Of course, these understandings are often shaken by experiences (Meadow 1980).

As an illustration, consider the following case: a well-educated couple, both of whom are teachers, both white, middle to upper income, and conventional in outlook, with virtually no knowledge of or contact with deaf people, discover that their one-year-old child is profoundly deaf. The couple lives within a small world that they have constructed from applied and accumulated knowledge about what being married and having a family means (Berger and Kellner 1964). When they discover that their child is deaf, or "hearing impaired," this knowledge, which they took for granted, has no apparent future use—it cannot unfold. In order to rear a child, they must assume that some mutual understanding takes place between them and their child. What they now know about their child has to be reconciled with what the parents thought they already knew about childrearing (see Meadow 1968, 1980).

Oralism as a formal system emerged to account for the presence of a deaf child in a hearing family in a way that would allow the parents to continue their understanding of parenthood *virtually unchanged*. This is another way of saying that oralism derives from ordinary cultural knowledge. It is an adaptation and a formalization of what everybody knows about normality. Asserting that equivalence between the hearing and the deaf is not only possible but also desirable allows the parents to continue, at least for a while and on occasion, to use their already existing knowledge about what it means to be parents: "My child is not 'deaf'. He just cannot 'hear'."

How this process works may be demonstrated by singling out some central understandings of common-sense knowledge of oralist parents. For instance, the idea that work produces results is crucial to most people's knowledge about life in our society; at least, this theme has been very strong in American culture (Merton 1963). From this we derive the maxim that virtually anything can be accomplished if only enough work is put into it. Although we may occasionally find skeptics—and, indeed, whole segments of modern society seem to live counter to this maxim (beatniks, hippies, and so forth)—most of us hold that work is the means to accomplishment.[1] Clearly, the oralists' exhortation that hard work and commitment are demanded of parents if they wish to achieve "success" bears a consistent relationship to this general cultural knowledge. Here success means that the children will be like the parents, or at least sufficiently similar so that the action of the children makes sense according to the parents' knowledge about being an acceptable person.

Parenthetically, we note that his dimension of mutual understanding, or misunderstanding, among hearing parents may actually contribute to the parents' guilt feelings. If it is taken for granted that hard work produces results and that others—one's friends or relatives—also operate according to this maxim, then lack of success (failure to get the child to speak normally) can mean (and is assumed by others to mean) that the parents are not working hard enough. Thus a circle is established that continually attributes blame for lack of success to the parents, who, regardless of how hard they work, fail to produce a "speaking" person like themselves. In fact, it can even be suggested that the more work done by the parents, the more guilty they feel. Within oralism, of course, the process just described dovetails with some parents' ideas about what might have caused deafness in the first place; for example, "We did something to cause this condition," or "We must have sinned and are being punished."

Filling in about Deafness

Another feature of interpretive procedures that will help us understand the endurance of ordinary assumptions in the meanings of deafness is often called the "et cetera" or "filling-in" assumption. This refers to a state of mind among people in social contact that allows them to let things pass despite their ambiguity or vagueness. In other words, once we presume a particular version of mutual understanding as a basis for social interaction, then, by assuming common knowledge and understandings, we can relieve ourselves of the obligation to define our terms or make explicit what those common experiences might be. For example, one person may be able reasonably to assume that he knows what the other means in order to go on with a conversation. The assumption is made that, if necessary, relevant information could be "filled in." For instance, when we meet a person we do not know well, there is always a period of conversation during which we have to establish a common understanding.[2] This is also true among signers: What does that sign mean; I sign that this way or that way; okay, now I see what you mean. After "I see what you mean," there is no necessity to fill in with a specific rendition of meaning for future use of that sign providing the parties remember their mutual understanding. Actually, as long as the receiver of the sign does not question the rendition, the conversation continues, even if both parties in fact have different backgrounds of experiences and relationships associated with the signs. This phenomenon, of course, occurs among users of oral languages as well. We are referring to the feelings or states of mind that parties to social interaction assume when they presume a common basis for communication. This is an ongoing process.

Once oralism functions as an interpretive procedure, then "sense" can be made out of deafness by allowing those operating within the policy to assume that filling in takes place. Oralism, as the term is used here, is a reconstructed view of what "normal talking" is like. It is a view that comes from commonsense knowledge rooted in a mainstream society. Once it becomes a way to interpret deafness, then it permits the operation of the same knowledge ordinarily used in everyday life. Consider that the distribution of causes of deafness is such that deaf children are found all along the continuum of economic well-being in American society. This means that many deaf children have middle-class parents. Deaf adults, as we shall show in subsequent chapters, customarily hold jobs that are manual, semiskilled, or skilled in nature, although increasing numbers are found in "underclass" white-collar occupations.

In the interesting situation presented here, hearing middle-class parents face a further discontinuity in their knowledge about childrearing. Parents almost always wish their children to be better off than they are or at least equal to themselves in terms of material well-being. If the deaf child is to succeed in his parents' view, he must reach the parents' station. This means that the child must pursue an occupation worthy of his background.

The dilemma posed by wanting the child to be better off, on the one hand, and knowing he is deaf, on the other, is aggravated by the parents' knowledge of the importance of using a linguistic style appropriate to a particular occupation. Parents know and assume that it is known by others that it is not enough merely to communicate in order to "make it" in the ordinary world. One must "talk" correctly, which often requires the use of a form of communication that is elaborate in style—a form that does not rest on presumptions about social context. In an elaborate style, words and sentences are used to convey subtle meanings that are not dependent on knowledge of the context of messages.

Bernstein (1971) and Robinson and Rackstraw (1972) have shown that lower-class people typically do not rely on such elaborate modes of communication. Rather, they communicate in ways that depend on prior knowledge of social situations. Their communication may be less complex both in form of sentences and in use of a variety of words. But this does not mean that their communication is less effective. It does mean, however, that much of the goal of elaborate communication is to display one's verbal skills. In fact, recently some linguists have taken great pains to show that middle-class talk is full of verbosity that usually adds nothing to the efficiency of communication (Labov 1970). When the display of such verbosity becomes a standard of occupational success, the deaf person is surely disadvantaged. The middle-class parent is intuitively aware of this disadvantage for his child.

However, among the working classes this kind of verbosity is less highly valued. Clear, straightforward communication to get a message across is more important than getting the message across with appropriate style; or, as, for example, in "bar talk," style may be highly circumscribed. The performance of sign language among the deaf, when compared with the performance of middle-class oral English, is less elaborate, less concerned with style, and more dependent on knowing the context to convey meaning. In general, there appears to be less difference between sign language and the version of English found among workers than between sign language and middle-class English at least on the dimension of style, a point we will develop further in chapter 4.

Thus oralism as a policy is an extension of the common-sense knowledge that middle-class persons already use in their everyday existence. An implication of this observation is that the tendency for private schools to be "oral" is not merely economic; an interesting relationship here is that the more expensive the school, the more likely it is that that school will be at least tacitly oral in policy. Conversely, the use of signs in public schools may be seen by many as a lowering of standards.

In another context, the same researchers mentioned previously provide some indirect evidence for these important class considerations. Bernstein and Henderson (1969) conducted a survey of what persons from various class backgrounds thought about the consequences of deafness. Middle-class persons believed that deafness and the presumed corresponding lack of oral facilities would be a serious block to developing personal relationships; working-class people, however, tended to place less stress on the personal aspects of a "language deficiency" and more on the way deafness might affect the learning of skills. This difference indicated that class background provides people in the respective classes with a knowledge about the importance of language. The middle class holds the belief that one who cannot talk surely cannot have friends or, perhaps more correctly, cannot learn to get what he or she wants from people by using language. For working-class people, interrelationships with other people seem to be less a linguistic matter. No wonder, then, that middle-class hearing parents stress the importance of learning to "talk," even to the extreme of depriving their children of close friendships.

Another set of assumptions that oralism draws from mainstream society is the knowledge of the usefulness of devices, equipment, and experts. Within the middle class it is taken for granted that problems either have or ought to have solutions. Solutions are offered in the form of "devices." Often these devices are linguistic (Scott and Lyman 1968), and oralism surely supplies its share of these: "You must realize it takes longer for these children to talk." "His eyes are too tired." "You don't talk to your child enough." Thus oralism has the power to relieve the necessity for understanding the social aspects of deafness by referring to the role of "special knowledge and its use." The parent does not have to try to understand what it is like to be deaf. All he has to do is refer to the application of devices by people who are supposed to know what they are doing—experts. The more equipment and the more technical the equipment, the better, because the less the parent is expected to do himself, the less he has to see the world through deaf eyes. The parents can let others tell them what to do. Certainly, placing hearing aids on small children is at least in part the result of this search for a device.

The oralist view of deafness is, then, a function of the distribution of common-sense knowledge in society. It promotes a way of communication that is consistent with common-sense understandings of being a competent person. What is not known is how much this perspective penalizes those who for one reason or another do not fit into the mold. We think it is safe to say that in many instances the view of deafness or the lack of it in the oralist interpretation is not consistent with the experience of being deaf.

Normal Forms and Normally Deaf

The final feature of interpretive procedures that we wish to discuss is the assumption with respect to *normal forms*. This refers to the presumption on the part of interacting persons that there exist certain normal appearances or typical understandings of acceptable appearances. Some authors have written of these as categories (Sacks 1972). Persons in interaction rely on their typical under-standings (categories) and assume that others share these understandings in order to make their surroundings seem recognizable. In American society, one such normal form is the common-sense notion that society holds together because of a sufficient amount of "sameness" among its members. With respect to talk, this becomes an understanding that all members of a given society speak in more- or less-appropriate ways, along with a correlative that outsiders likewise show their sameness through the use of argots. Extending this notion to evaluations already made, we arrive at an appraisal that success in the society rests on an individual's achievement of this sameness.

If something such as a physical handicap interfere with literal equivalence, then success is measured by how close one can come to being like others. In other words, approximations are made to what is thought of as an ideal state. As already pointed out, these presumptions are not necessarily the actual forms of understanding among those who are regarded as having succeeded. For example, a study of deaf persons in professional employment shows that the ability to produce normal speech was of secondary importance for relationships between the deaf and their hearing coworkers in the opinion of the deaf people (Crammatte 1968). Likewise, many of these successful deaf people reported that they were only poor to fair lipreaders. Thus oralism provides a distorted version of what deaf persons may actually rely on in communication with hear-ing coworkers. The everyday world of the deaf contrasts with the common-sense understandings of the everyday world of successful middle-class people.

Reconstructions of what deaf people really need bears no similarity to, or at least confuses correspondence with, the structures of the deaf world. The typification of society that holds that all must be alike in order to be together denies the deaf child access to the negotiation of the meaning of his own exis-tence in society. It provides him with categories for producing meanings that are not his but are, rather, those of his parents, who assume experiences that the child simply does not have. Surely, educational policies grounded in oralism may even promote self-crises by confronting the deaf child with what is at best a translation of an elaborate, context-free communicative mode for making sense of one's surroundings into a highly contextually restricted version of teacher-parent dependency for expression and understanding.

In conclusion, deafness is first and foremost a social phenomenon. Its meaning is the result of an interplay of views that are usually associated with two distinct sets of biographies and experiences: on the one hand, hearing people trying to make sense out of deafness without changing their basis for understanding social competency and, on the other hand, deaf people trying to live within a hearing society. How deafness is understood, especially for hearing parents of deaf children, is largely a matter of application of already available knowledge. English-based policies account for deafness by drawing on widely distributed understandings that are already strong in society. When oralist programs fail to produce "normally achieving adults," that failure may be judged as the direct consequence of the strength of the interpretation, since the interpretation itself is often at odds with the realities of being deaf. Ultimately, what seems to be most important to oralists is that their understanding of what society is like not be changed by the presence of a deaf person. This is reasonable from their point of view. That changes in deaf education are taking place—Meadow (1980) refers to the changes of the last ten years as revolutionary—is an indication that tolerance of differences in society may be increasing. But it remains to be seen whether this is a genuine change that will accommodate the needs of the deaf even when those needs conflict with the ordinary understandings of what society is like.

Notes

1. Merton (1963) would suggest that such strains between unattainable goals and institutionally given means will foster "deviant" adaptations. Hence, parents may ritualize by clinging to the techniques of language instruction or may retreat by scaling down their goals for their offspring; they could, further, become politically active in attempts to promote innovative means of achieving full participation in society for their children; or, finally, they could rebel by clashing with societal and cultural forces in an effort to change the very organization of interaction between the hearing and deaf. In chapter 5 we deal explicitly with these and other types of adaptations.

2. This observation is supported, at least indirectly, by voice-onset-time studies that indicate that people do not understand each other through the perception of discrete bits of language information. Rather, we perceive a pattern or *gestalt* within the limits of human auditory modalities (Lieberman 1975). We would expect that there are visual limitations to the recognition of patterns as well, and that a sign language would conform to these patterns, albeit within broader ranges of distribution. (See Siple 1978; Stevens and House 1955).

4

The Consciousness of Deafness: Class Patterns

By *consciousness* we mean an individual's aware use of systems of common-sense knowledge. We have pointed out that such systems serve as the baseline of interaction, and that consciousness, as comprising the mental processes of intentional interpretation, is a typical feature of all social organization (Psathas 1973; Weigert 1975). What content does the form of deaf consciousness assume? How might it be described, and what relationship does it bear to larger societal structures?

To address these questions implied in earlier chapters, we will describe two predominant features of modern society and then offer a portrait of the consciousness of deafness. Using available ethnographic information, we will sketch the content and form of middle-class and lower-class consciousness. Then, using the concept of social distance, we will contrast the consciousness of the deaf with these.

The Consciousness of the Middle Class

In politics, appearance, religion, and virtually every other aspect of everyday life, Americans gravitate toward an imagined "golden mean." There is a dilemma within this tendency, however. On the one hand, we wish to avoid being extremely different from those we judge to be our equals; on the other, we wish to preserve for ourselves a unique identity. A classic problem in sociological analysis, appropriately, has been to explain how social order is achieved both in spite of and by way of a strong individualistic ideology (Lyman and Scott 1970; Mills 1959). Many critics have exposed the disdain in which Americans hold communal existence.[1] It is as if groups with strong ethnic, racial, linguistic, or class hegemony embarrass us by uncovering our dilemma. Typically, we fail to understand how individualism can be experienced within community solidarity; and we tolerate only the most-indirect and necessary constraints on our lives (see Stack 1974; Parker 1973).

Most Americans call themselves "middle-class," although economic, racial, and ethnic realities produce great disparities among the population, with a skewed distribution of our scarcest reward—money—toward the middle of the bottom end of a class array. For example, using Colman and Neugarten's (1971) criteria, a full 89 percent of our population can be classified at or below the "middle class": lower-middle class (32 percent), upper-lower class (39 percent), and lower-lower class (18 percent). The most-recent research supports these general proportions.

Minimally, we can conclude that the ideology of class and its economics do not match perfectly. Years ago, Lloyd Warner and his colleagues pointed out that the interpretation of economic resources is as important as their possession. Class consciousness is a matter of both resources and their use according to prevailing standards of civility (see Warner 1960).

We have broached a subject that is covered by a voluminous literature. Fortunately, our aim delimits this literature and focuses on a task of analytic description. We know, first, that people think in highly individualistic ways about their money and what to do with it. Second, we know that what they do with it and whether they have it at all or in sufficient amounts influences their life chances and styles (Rainwater 1974). We also know that people's intentional interpretations—their consciousnesses—are both creative of and constricted by their location within an overall structure, a class system. That there is an interplay among these constricted interpretations allows us to address questions of patterned meanings.

Middle-class consciousness can be described according to four features: (1) attitudes toward and uses of language; (2) styles of communication in the expression of values and emotions; (3) attitudes toward material well-being; and, finally, (4) a typical common-sense reasoning procedure that forms the foundation of a world view.[2] We suggest that within this view there exists sufficient latitude to allow individuals to draw the conclusion that they are "masters of their own destiny," whereas the organization of the view functions in itself to outline a common symbolic universe or a set of "we-relations."

It is important to reiterate that we are discussing consciousness and not actual economic well-being. Further, we focus on the essential forms of that consciousness. This problem has been formulated in various ways. For example, we can think of it in terms of conventional sociological theory, as a matter of "unanticipated consequences of social action" where we are less concerned with the enjoining of specific actions of economic well-being (the objective consequences) than "with the subjective satisfaction of duty well performed" (Merton 1974, p. 154)—the unanticipated consequences. Rather than identifying descriptive attributes of class action, we are abstracting the core values, which, of course, may be coupled in very complex relationships with sometimes contradictory courses of action.

The Proper Use of English

A person's values toward language represent one hallmark of consciousness about status:

> Dialect may have an objective reality in the way people talk, but it seems quite clear that it at the same time has subjective reality in the kinds of consistent attitudes which people hold toward one another's speech. [Shuy and Fasold 1973, p. 95]

The goal of upwardly mobile speech is to demonstrate "proper" use of the mother tongue or the standard variant of the dominant language.

Although the relationship between socioeconomic variables and language is not as strong as that between ethnicity or race and language, the literature does suggest that the use of standard linguistic forms is associated with middle-class, upwardly mobile persons, either white or black. Research has repeatedly demonstrated that speech evokes "stereotypical" or common-sense categories of interpretation (Shuy and Fasold 1973). This means that, conversely, the control of dialect (accent, lexicon, and syntax) can be an important avenue of movement within a social system.

Middle-class mothers expand the truncated expressions of their children into "models" of English (Brown and Bellugi 1964). In many homes there is a perpetual war between the influences of peers or uncritical neighbors of lower status and the parents' idea of the right way to speak. Reflexively, a parent "corrects" a double negative, points out that *ain't* is not a word, or deletes a superflous *s* from *anyways*.

There is no doubt that the middle class acts on the presumption that there is a standard form of English. Perhaps the most-dramatic illustration of this comes from parental responses to the introduction of certain nonstandard dialects into the classroom. Among black middle-class parents of school-age children, one often encounters a strong resistance to the use of "black English," or at least to its use in instructional settings. One prominent black educator recently said that there is no such thing as black English. Rather, he said, there is only proper or improper English; black people must learn the "correct" use of their language. To bring the slang of the street into the classroom does a great disservice to the child by simply creating a false impression that his way of speaking is correct.[3]

Ardent supporters of traditional curricula in the schools are often those recently arrived in the middle class and those who assess their life chances as being extremely precarious. They have clear mental images of the instruments of mobility, and chief among these is the "proper use of the language of society."

For the person with fixed notions of what is standard, how one speaks is the medium par excellence of the impression one gives. Not only is the mastery of correct grammar important for cognitive style, but it is also essential for personhood itself. What comes out of the mouth may, indeed, defile. And the worst slip of the tongue is that which betrays a social origin below the status aspired to or attained.

In middle-class consciousness, standard English embodies the horizons of social experience. Certainly, the range of actual experiences is vast. As Bensman and Vidich (1971) write, there are many innovative variations on middle-class themes, such as "radical chic," "culture-vultures," and the attempts of the lower middle classes to absorb the newer life-styles. All these experiences, however, in varying degrees and intensities, unfold within a presumption of a linguistic form.

Stylistic Variations

English is used as a vernacular; and, as several scholars have demonstrated, there are styles to such a vernacular. Joos (1961) identified styles ranging from the intimacy of dyadic interactions, through casual talk among friends, to styles of formal and consultative discourse. Syntax, lexicon, and semantics vary with stylistic shifts. In a sociology of language these shifts indicate not only the range of an individual's social versatility but also qualitative differences in types of social interchanges. In a widely cited paper, Scott and Lyman (1968) show that whether others honor a person's account of an untoward act depends in part on that person's skill in selecting an appropriate style within which the content of talk can be framed. Thus low-status persons may be hypercorrect or excuse their behavior on social grounds but may commit linguistic improprieties when offering accounts to a superior (see Labov 1970).

In American middle-class culture there is a hierarchy of stylistic variation. Intimate and casual styles generally are regarded as important for private life, whereas formal styles are appropriate for public affairs. Since sharper and more-enforceable distinctions are made between public and private affairs in modern, middle-class society, and since public—particularly rational—discourse assumes increasing importance, we see that the typical middle-class person develops competence disproportionately in *formal* styles of discourse. Among the middle classes intimate and casual styles are situationally specific, usually emotional in content, and rarely intended for public use.

Bernstein's (1972) research on code usages further informs us about this feature of middle-class consciousness when coupled with available empirical studies. Surveys of attitudes toward nonstandard dialects of English (Taylor 1973) reveal a surprising range of acceptance of "situationally appropriate" use of such dialects. Attitudes, however, vary systematically with ethnic identity. Among teachers, for example, blacks generally tend to be more receptive than white teachers to the use of black English in all kinds of interactional situations. (Nevertheless, as noted earlier, in this attitude teachers may be atypical of middle-class black families.) Still, as Bernstein suggests, the middle class is proficient at code switching from, in his terms, "elaborate" to "restricted" usages. In Joos's terms (1961), although there are other distinctions to be made in this comparison, switching takes place between "formal-consultative" and "intimate-casual" styles. The chief difference between these code variations seems to be a semantic one. Restricted variants require broad-ranging assumptions about common experiences, whereas elaborate performances function to circumscribe the boundaries of assumptions necessary to the "realization of meaning" (Bernstein 1972).

A person socialized into a middle-class life-style will push toward standard-variant usage as topics of discourse become more public, whereas lower-class persons will persist in the usage of nonstandard or dialect variants, regardless of the topic being discussed. In order to talk seriously, therefore, the middle-class speaker will move toward "formal-elaborate" organization of talking, whereas his or her lower-class counterpart may attempt to approximate "formal" variants. Because of the communal nature of their socialization experiences, however, these variants will be *restricted* to vernaculars of class. Middle-class consciousness allows for individualistic variable use of language according to a differentiated cognitive style (see Parsons 1951).

Material Well-Being as a Model of Success

In his examination of the meaning of the "success motif" in American life, Merton (1963) showed that the uneven distribution of opportunities to achieve success—given the relatively even distribution of the belief about its importance —could generate deviant behavior in a population. Warner (1960), Lynd and Lynd (1929), and Williams (1970) showed what ingenious interpretations of success people could concoct and how these interpretations are often associated with the so-called objective features of well-being.

How people cope with truncated resources has been a topic of much of the best sociological research of the last decade. Rainwater (1974), for example, shows how the absence of money translates into a variety of illnesses—financial, physical, and psychological. Stack (1974) documents the complexities of strategies of survival as they have become institutionalized into a kind of ambivalent dependence on the "welfare system." This literature, through direct description of middle-class consciousness and through contrast of middle- and lower-class life-styles, allows for the distillation of the characteristic meanings of material well-being in American society.

Persons of middle-class consciousness see technological advances as means to achieve higher states of well-being. Although they may experience some anxiety toward increasingly complex information systems and toward high technology in general, middle-class people are generally predisposed to interpret increased, technological complexity as advancement. The naive "progressivism" of some early-twentieth-century minds has given way to cautious attitudes about the increasing complexity of everyday life. Even within the middle class itself there are slivers of resistance to newer and better gadgetry. Still, liberation from the forces of both nature and man is typically seen as a consequence of technology. Women become free to participate in mainstream societal affairs when they have mastery over their biological selves. The new community, Toufler (1980) observes, will be constructed from nuclei of electroic cottages. All humankind ultimately depends on a wise but nevertheless complete dominion over nature.

This way of thinking leads to an admiration for the new and the complicated and leads one to place faith in rational discourse and energetic goal-oriented behavior. Technological development embodies this "natural attitude." From solid-state, direct-drive turntables to alternative systems of energy, the future is viewed with a kind of cautious optimism. The "future" means more mastery of nature and more human control.

The popular television program "Buck Rogers of the Twenty-fifth Century" introduced a deaf character into one episode in the 1979-1980 season. The presence of this deaf girl in a future so advanced that diseases of our era like cancer, heart ailments, and systemic failures are remembered only as the problems of less-well-developed medical sciences was explained by reference to her isolation from "modern" medical capacities. Her contact with twenty-fifth-century civilization is ameliorated by Buck's knowledge of signs, a knowledge of the past. But in the end her dependence on signs and Buck's knowledge of them are reduced again to historical curiosities as the girl undergoes "electronic surgery" and "extensive retraining" in order to become normal.

A theme closely related to the ideal of progress is that of movement on a ladder of success. So much has been written about this belief that we need only sketch its generalities. One's first job is considered a starting place, not a fixture in a career. Movement from job to job implies a better-to-best succession.

Sociologists have recently talked of *situs*, meaning a layering of occupations to form a set that can be objectively described as being above or below another situs. Lateral movement within a situs may be what really happens in American society, but to admit this—or, worse, to notice downward movement—evokes responses of shame, pity, and outrage.

Although modern society has produced an amazing variety of styles of entrepreneurship (see Kruger's 1979 treatment of "hip capitalism"), the requisite of work remains. In the retelling of a success story, luck, circumstance, and social fate give way to effort, opportunism, ingenuity, and persistence. In middle-class consciousness the individual must finally come to terms with "self" and must be willing to act, to do more than simply be. We have seen the impact of the countercultural values of the hippies in modifying this aspect of consciousness. However, as Irwin (1977) and others have shown, although this impact may be substantial, a "deep structure"—a bedrock feature of our interpretation of the meanings of our everyday lives—remains essential.

All this recent discovery of the "individualized" meaning of success points to a consciousness that Bernstein captures in the term *person orientation.*

In his effort to specify the "formally framed contexts" of speech, he delineates characteristics of a middle-class family where

> the relationships become more egocentric and the unique attitudes of family members more and more substantive. . . . Such families do not reduce but increase the substantive expression of ambiguity and ambivalence. [Bernstein 1972, p. 174]

The achievement of any clarity of meaning in relationships within the context of middle-class consciousness depends on the cognitive and linguistic abilities of its members to make sense out of complicated, emerging, and often ad hoc negotiations of roles within a highly amorphously defined social structure. Certainly, the so-called natural attitude of the middle class places an emphasis on the person as the fundamental unit of social order.

The interpretive procedures embodied within the natural attitude of middle-class consciousness display an organization that can be fixed. To recognize a potential partner in discourse is to attribute to that person a similar "thought process" and character. In the vernacular, to know that one's partner in interaction has "gotten it together" is a necessary condition of person-oriented exchanges.

As Bernstein suggests, this means that it is less important to know what kind of person one is about to engage than to know what this person *will do*. Can the person recognize a situationally appropriate behavior? a clue that a private domain has been breached? In short, civility itself rests on a highly sophisticated bifurcation of the self into private and public sectors. This leads, perforce, to the constant interpretation of intentions on the basis of appearance. In his caustic style, Mills (1951) portrayed one consequence of this person orientation—that America itself has become a "great salesroom":

> The personality-market, the most decisive effect and symptom of the great salesroom, underlies the all pervasive distrust and self-alienation so characteristic of metropolitan people. . . . Men are estranged from one another as each secretly tries to make an instrument of the other, and in time a full circle is made: one makes an instrument of himself and is estranged from it also. [Mills 1951, pp. 187-188]

In the middle-class natural attitude, language is an instrument of interaction that, ironically, is used to seek more and more depersonalized, standard and invariant forms. As less of the self is defined as private, the organization of "membership discourse" becomes less appropriate for general interactional purposes. Material well-being becomes both more individualistically defined and more negotiable, open to alternative interpretations. As a credit to the constantly changing roles an individual plays in the drama of modern society, a person becomes the object of manipulation. Consequently, the sense of community that one is capable of experiencing becomes weaker, paler, and more malleable than the old hierarchies of social organization.

Lower-Class Points of View as Residuals of Premodern Consciousness

A remarkable insight developed in several recent books (Berger, Berger, and Kellner 1973: Cuddihy 1974) is that the processes of modernization do not proceed evenly within any society and that pockets of consciousness can exist relatively untouched by what we have characterized as the middle-class natural attitude. This way of talking about consciousness allows us to describe the distribution of features of natural attitudes according to their conformity to standard interpretations of the meanings of everyday life. The foregoing account stresses how standardization and segmentalization go hand in hand. The exceedingly rich literature on communities or "unmodern" ways of life within the general context of modern society allows us to contrast natural attitudes. Whether these attitudes are black, Italian, blue collar, or whatever, they have distinctive and essential components.

First, nonstandard-language variant forms embody the horizons of experience for the members of these *unmodern* communities. Although there are differentiated usages of variants, the patterns of use by social class seem clear enough: members of the lower classes, black and white, male and female, whether they are aware of it or not, use nonstandard forms in everyday interactions more often than do their white or black, male or female, middle-class counterparts (see Trudgill 1974, pp. 91-102). These nonstandard variants range from vernacular to dialectic to pidgin among the various segments of the American speech community. The essential observation for our purposes is that these variegated sociolinguistic phenomena suggest equally distinct interpretive procedures. The people who take these forms for granted, as the ordinary medium for social exchange live in unique symbolic spheres. In their versions of life's significance or the lack of it, they start from a different place than do middle-class people.

Bernstein has argued that such different origins reflect general patterns of socialization. The lower classes use a semantic system that is sensitive to common experiences; or, at least, the presumption of common experiences engenders speech that is relatively more context bound than that of the middle classes. He identifies what he refers to as a *restricted code* for communication. This code operates through the sophisticated use of a *referential* system. Certainly, not all nonstandard variants are restricted codes; but Bernstein's research and that of others (Lawton 1968; Robinson and Rackstraw 1972) does seem to demonstrate that a preponderance of such code usage is associated with tightly defined kinship structures and heightened sense of community (see Stack 1974).

Stylistic Variations

We have, then, two important observations that are separate but mutually reinforcing in their implications for understanding a "deaf class consciousness." First, class and nonstandard language uses are associated; second, there are distinctive stylistic ranges within class strata. Whereas middle-class speakers surely employ a wide-ranging stylistic repertoire, their facilities with intimate and casual styles pale by comparison with the lexical, syntactical, and socio-linguistic complexity of lower-class vernaculars and dialects.

Labov's extensive work on the "ritual insult"—the sound—used by young black males illustrates this point. Although whites also use the ritual insult, the forms they employ are essentially a limited set of routines, "whereas the black practice of sounding ranges over a wide variety of forms and topics which are combined with great flexibility" (Labov 1974, p. 95).

Although he makes no effort to preserve the "sounds of blue-collar aristo-crats" when relating materials quoted from interviews with patrons of the Oasis bar, E.E. Le Masters (1975, pp. 36, 49) does convey a sense of the flavor and vitality of tavern talk. A happily married woman retorts, "My husband is a real nice bastard" Or an older couple talks about their life together: "You know, professor, Bob and me have never had an argument in our forty years of mar-riage," to which the husband, Bob, replies, "That's a lot of bullshit—what are you trying to do, feed the professor a lot of crap?"

The literature on the linkage between ethnic identities and speech com-munities is vast and convincing (Fishman 1972). It seems safe to summarize this research as follows: Among the middle classes, although the range of stylistic variation in speech is wide, the development of competency within the various categories of the array remains relatively simple. But within more dis-tinctively describable speech communities (ethnic neighborhoods, racially defined peer groups, occupational groupings with strong class identities), the range of stylistic variability can be characterized as narrow and complex; that is, the nonstandard variants may circumscribe the range of styles truncating formal and consultant versions while enriching the vernaculars of everyday life.

Success Motif

The value of success is well known and widely espoused by the middle classes, and the mass media portray success as "all American" (Rainwater 1966, p. 25). But this does not warrant the conclusion that, at least at the social-psycholog-ical level, the value is distributed equally among members of objectively defined classes. Hyman (1953) and later Rainwater (1966) demonstrate that substantial differences exist in attitudes about the meanings of home, education, and jobs; about the risks that one should be willing to take to achieve success; and about the opportunities one can expect to find throughout life. As we would expect from Merton's theoretical insights, among middle-class persons there is a general fit between an individual's relative success and his or her endorsement of the "all-American package." Among the lower classes, people's attitudes seem to reflect the objective reality of there socioeconomic existence.

Recent research has indicated that mainstream values do, in fact, penetrate the lower classes, where the sense that is made out of them is conditioned by the nature of the sociocultural context of poverty. Certainly, Rodman (1963) shows that urban blacks apply mainstream values in their lives, even if in a somewhat distorted version. Stack (1974) informs us that

> mainstream values have failed many residents of the Flats [the black community she studied]. Nevertheless, the life ways of the poor present a powerful challenge to the notion of a self-perpetuating culture of poverty. The strategies that the poor have evolved to cope with poverty do not compensate for poverty · in themselves, nor do they perpetuate the poverty cycle. But when mainstream values fail the poor . . . the harsh conditions of poverty force people to return to proven strategies for survival. [1974, p. 129]

Both the meanings of success and the opportunities available to pursue it are conditioned by the ongoing character of social organization in the objectively defined life-styles of individuals. Still, values persist even while adaptive strategies emerge. For us, this means that the familiar success motif is often weak and is surely interpreted according to indigenous values and attitudes and to the necessities of economic survival among the members of the lowest socioeconomic strata in American society.

Interactive modes reflect these conditions, giving rise to networks that can be "tenacious, active and lifelong". Again, Bernstein's logic seems appropriate. He contends that members of the lower classes think in terms of common experiences. (Residents of the Flats spoke of "what goes round comes round," and referred to people as "those you count on.") A vital sense of community is often at odds with general values of individualism. Although this sense of oneness provides strength to survive together in the face of adversity it may be a burden in that one may be unable to seize the opportunity, if one does occur, to move up. As Hyman put it, "if the individual regarded his chances to achieve his goal as negligible, when in reality they were good, there would be a psychologically produced strain toward deviance" (1953, p. 484). Of course, as contemporary literature shows, relationships are interpreted in ways that give rise to lifetime obligations, which, in turn, may result in "regarding chances to achieve as negligible."

Deaf Consciousness

Deaf people interpret the world according to certain typical ways of thinking. This observation must not be taken as a statistical generalization. Instead, it is a characterization, or ideal typical description, designed to identify a pattern of consciousness. People who cannot hear come from all walks of life and all stations in society—daughters of opera singers, sons of movie stars, the offspring of carpenters and welfare mothers. Nevertheless, so magnetic is the pull of the "deaf community," so pervasive its impact, that we can suggest the validity of a "patterned set of actions"—deaf actions. There is a typical way of interpreting the meanings of everyday life that is available to those who cannot hear; Its forms, although not all use them, are known to all deaf persons and frame the meanings of their lives.

We stress that we are aiming for the typical and that we are dealing with the confounding influences of broader, more widely distributed knowledge systems. This confounding results in a complex mosaic of consciousness that includes ethnic, racial, sexual, and class variations. However, the essential frame of deaf consciousness can be described. We offer the following sketch.

The meanings of everyday life are embodied in American Sign Language (ASL), which, minimally, must be regarded as a nonstandard linguistic form within the American speech community. As previous researchers have indicated, there are two senses in which ASL is nonstandard: (1) as an indigenous, non-foreign, yet alien language, and (2) as a pidginized variant of English, more accurately a creole. Either approach allows the conclusion that ASL is non-standard from the perspective of the wider community.

Stylistic variations in the use of sign are narrow and complex. That is, considerable style-form variation has been identified in sign from intimate, highly contextually sensitive practical examples, as in children's use of sign in the dormitories of residential schools for the deaf or in more formally constrained variations in the prose and poetics of the theatrical medium (Klima and Bellugi 1979). The differences in style forms are great, given the limited range of social contexts for the use of sign. Compare, for example, the range of stylistic use in English found in a typical middle-class male speaker's performances. Morning interactions at the family breakfast table could be intimate and casual; contact with familiar people at the corner drugstore or the barbershop might be carried on in a casual form; office business and important matters of planning and counseling might be transacted in standard forms or even through the artificial variants found in bureaucracy (see Hummel 1978). Although similar variations can be located within the sign-using community itself, in sheer numbers alone the range of use could be expected to be greater for the middle-class speaker.

Still, as we contended earlier, the variations are largely lexical and phonological and are measurably less-complicated differences, than is a sign shift from friendly interaction with someone well known to interaction with a new, unknown signer of higher putative social status.

The success motif is weak within deaf consciousness, and attitudes toward it are ambivalent. A successful deaf man is sorely underemployed in comparison to his hearing counterpart; and, with exceptions duly noted, the aspirations of the deaf with regard to their chances for success in the wider society are tempered by realism in their appraisals of the obstacles at hand.

As Hyman (1953) documented, one's position in relation to the perceived top of the social ladder is reflected in an individual's interpretation of opportunities to succeed. A deaf child prefaces his anticipation of success with the question, "Can a deaf person be. . .?" Can a deaf person be a major-league baseball player, a doctor, a trial lawyer, a college president, a principal of a school?

Just as a ghetto child takes on the attitudes of the adults around him toward the limits of success for a black person in a white world, so the deaf child sooner or later learns the restraints of deafness on participation in the American dream.

Two avenues of interpretation open, each with different consequences. First, aspirations can be allowed to soar as the deaf person reaches for the impossible dream. The very few who succeed are praised, and the rest are left with shattered dreams and strong feelings of inadequacy. This path has been well worn by the hearing, whose journeys have been chronicled by sociologists pointing to the excesses of their egoism.

Second—and surely similar to the strategies of adaptation adopted by the disadvantaged in society—is the scaling down of lofty cultural goals. Such modification in the very means and goals of society and culture results in the distinctive life-styles associated with certain conditions of social existences—with being black, poor, female, or handicapped.

As we have already observed, a corollary to the adaptive avenue is the strength of communal experience, the enchantment of shared grief, through which one gains a sense of worth from one's place within a larger collective entity. Disproportionate attention to the cause-and-effect role of individual effort can divert criticism from broader issues of organization that have more-direct relevance to the disadvantaged person's experience.

Story telling, a kind of oral tradition, seems to play a crucial role in the consciousness of the deaf. The extent of the symbolic boundaries of deafness is vast. Hence, the murder of the hearing parents of a well-known deaf woman, married to a deaf man and with deaf children, becomes the occasion for shared grief among the community. There is much telling and retelling of the how's and why's, much discussion of the senselessness of the act. There is a large turnout at the funeral—many deaf people mourning the parents of a friend. These parents did not sign; in life, they were merely courteously accepted. In death, however, they come under the symbolic structure of the meanings of deafness. Such a phenomenon of "mourning by association" seems out of place in a segmentalized modern society in which the death of those outside one's immediate family often has little emotional impact.

Social Distance

Although the concept of social distance is usually thought of in connection with the measurement of perceived proximity among "significant groupings" of people (see Bogardus 1925), the concept has a phenomenological aspect as well. People place one another in social space. The idea of proximity is part of a person's "natural attitude." As we have argued, social space takes on properties according to the knowledge people have of it; that is, it is reflexively created and sustained by continuous application of knowledge.

We have outlined features of that space in terms of one of its many dimensions, class consciousness. Cultural space, an abstraction of common-sense knowledge as applied by a group of people bound in history and place, may be described. Further, within it relationships can be identified and used as explanatory devices for locating the observations of a specific character within an overall scheme.

In a person's natural attitude, ideas of space operate to rank categories of people in terms of nearness to the group in which one assumes membership. To the extent that our descriptions encompass the distinctions members would make both within and about the space they have created for the unfolding of their everyday lives, we can introduce analytic remarks or hypotheses about spatial arrangements.

There is less social distance between hearing persons of the lower classes and members of other lower-class life-styles than between either hearing persons of the middle classes and those of the lower classes or between hearing middle-class persons and the deaf.

As a maxim this statement has far-reaching implications. It highlights a middle-class bias toward standard forms. It identifies ranges of stylistic variation that are class bound. It places the deaf within broader structures of society. It dramatizes what Merton called the *ambivalency* that can be built into social roles. In metaphorical terms hearing parents must deal with a breach in their spatial arrangements of everyday life according to class meanings as they decide continuously what it means to have a deaf offspring. Conversely, the deaf person born to middle-class parents grows older into a "lower" stratum and harbors simultaneously the tastes of an individualistic, segmentalized, private/public, literate, middle-class world and the nonliterate, communal, unmodern folkways of the deaf.

Such a life situation manifests an "approach-avoidance" dynamic that plays itself out in every aspect of hearing-deaf exchanges: The cordiality that the deaf extend to the hearing is coupled with distrust, especially for the hearing signer; the desire to be included in mainstream society is tempered by the solace that derives from being in the company of one's own kind.

We have sought to depict an interpretive nexus that reflects ambivalence in its very symbolic structure. Thus, mainstreaming, oralism, and emphasis on the use of English should be symbolic of the middle classes, along with the placement of a stigma on the use of hands, expressions, and gestures. Bowling, labor unions, beer, sports, and sharp male-female divisions of labor are "deaf" characteristics; theater, equalitarianism, radical political expression, and innovative forms of everyday life are not! A *hearing* infrastructure emphasizes higher education; and a *hearing* literati pushes and sustains innovative, higher-order endeavors. Thus, in a sense, the hearing "front" for the deaf. The activities of the deaf community seem profiled by a different spatial configuration from those of the middle class—one more like that of the families of the Flats (as studied by Stack (1974) or of the men and women of LeMaster's (1975) Oasis Bar. However, the colors that shade this portrait of deaf space or its consciousness are not coordinated. Instead, they clash, their brilliance melting into gray tones of ambivalence and marginality.

Notes

1. In his recent popular book, Gay Talese (1980) carefully documents societal reaction to the communal movements of the early midnineteenth century. Among Fourierists, Mormons, or members of the Oneida community, to name only a few, conventional reaction played significant roles in the modification and demise of most of their communal efforts. More recently, the proliferation of communes that apparently peaked in the early 1970s has continued to elicit controlling responses from the larger society (Talese 1980, pp. 300-353).

Many ethnographies of racially and ethnically cohesive communities have stressed the strength these experiences impart to their members (Stack 1974). In an unpublished paper Parker (1973) writes about the uniqueness of the individual within the black community, particularly in socialization experiences, describing the way in which one can be different and still belong to a family or group.

The process of naming (nicknames); the noncompetitive character of family life; and such rituals as "signifying," "ribbing," and the like, according to Parker, prepares a person for dealing with the white world; reinforce a sense of belonging to the collective identity; and, at the same time, instill a sense of individualism. These socialization tactics are largely absent or less than central in white, middle-class families, where the emphasis is instead on "finding oneself" within a complex range of alternative occupational and educational options.

2. We use the term *world view* to refer to sets of assumptions, loosely associated and often dispersive, that an individual uncritically calls on to appraise the overall qualities of his or her social existence—that is, the most-general meanings of the most broadly conceived boundaries of personal experience (see Gouldner 1970, pp. 30-33; Wagner 1970).

3. This passage is a paraphrase from a lecture delivered by Dr. Benjamin Mays to a class at Macalester College, 1980.

5 Hearing Parents of Deaf Children: A Typological Analysis

Meadow (1980, pp. 145-146) writes that total communication has been so extensively adopted in elementary and preschool programs for the hearing impaired that it amounts to a "revolution." The oral, day-school program, once the most-common response to the needs of deaf children has become virtually a relic. Since parents are influenced by the advice they receive and by the educational opportunities available to them, strict or totally oral parents also are becoming less common. However, our research reveals that the assumptions from which parents operate still revolve around attitudes toward spoken English and the deaf experience. Further, we have observed, as have others (Erting 1980), that the actual signing of hearing parents bears little resemblance to American Sign Language and that, perhaps in most cases, children of such parents must rely on nonverbal clues and on whatever mastery of spoken English they can achieve. Hence, the typology developed here is properly seen as having less to do with actual behavior than with the ways in which parents interpret having a deaf offspring.

The definitive considerations for identifying types of parents are (1) the parent's attitudes toward using their hands according to some systematic language-like rules and (2) their evaluation of the deaf experience.[1] The actual modes of communication employed by parents vary from complete reliance on speech (speech reading and speech production) to the use of signs only, that is, signs without lip movements or other speech-based nonverbal techniques. Evaluations of the deaf experience range from accepting it as a unique, but normal, way of life (the deaf community) to placing a stigma on not hearing (see Meadow and Nemon 1976).

These dimensions define two basic types: (1) *oralists,* who regard various forms of manual communication as irrelevant to their own personal and family environments; and (2) *signers,* who espouse the use of some type of manual communication system. The oralist category contains three subtypes: recruiter, searcher, and aloof. Signers, likewise, may be subdivided into three subtypes: parents who see the deaf as handicapped and capable of only limited accomplishments (the "all-they-can-do" type), sign changers, and friends of the deaf.

This chapter is a revised and expanded version of Jeffrey Nash, "Hearing Parents of Deaf Children: A Typology," *Sign Language Studies* (Summer 1975):163-180. Used with permission of Linstok Press.

Characteristics of Oralist Types

Oralists bring to the situation of having a nonhearing child the same background knowledge and common-sense assumptions that exist in society in general. Separate dimensions of knowledge, forms of consciousness, and other culturally defined experiences are often regarded as irrelevant to "proper" communication within the present-day world. The world view of the oralists may be simply described: there is an acknowledged, indisputable mode for interpreting the world in practical, everyday terms. That mode requires all five senses, and all participants are presumed to sense things in the same way.[2] Any complete social knowledge must derive from a complete sensory base. With a regard to communication, a maxim emerges: No normal talking, no normal social interaction.

Oralists interpret the status hierarchy of the society as a system allowing upward movement and accumulation of wealth.[3] Given their child's impairment, oralists—always operating from the criteria given by mainstream society—judge success in terms of his or her approximation to the ideal. Their children's language is judged by how closely it resembles the speech of hearing people and whether or not the child can "talk to anyone." The goal of these parents is to integrate their children into a hearing world. Their child's behavior and general social performance is evaluated by the same criteria they would employ for a normal child. The deaf child must therefore approximate "normality," and full normality depends on the restoration of hearing at some future time.

To oralist parents, sign language is regarded as a form of communication not appropriate to sophisticated or cultivated communication. They rank languages on a continuum on which signs are mere "gestures" and "fingerspelling"—an awkward and embarrassingly slow imitation of spoken English. Their tolerant acceptance of signs for those who "need" them does not alter their relegation of signs to a remedial station. To oralists, manual communication is inferior to verbal communication, a last resort used only when a child is hopelessly handicapped. They attempt to avoid or postpone this judgment in the case of their own children, and acquiesce to the use of signs only for other children whose parents they see as not capable of teaching, nurturing, and shouldering the burden of a "hearing-impaired" child.

The Recruiters

Bob and Sally are college graduates. Bob is a personnel manager for a large oil company, Sally is a housewife. She is an active woman. Before the birth of their child, she was the rising star of the Junior League and the League of Women Voters, and chief organizer of the gourmet club. Bob is a toastmaster and a member of the Junior Chamber of Commerce. Although they are still active in these associations, their energies

Table 5-1
Typological Depiction of Hearing Parents of Deaf Children

Types of Parents	Manual Communication		Deaf Experience		Within Comparisons		Between Comparisons	
	Self Relevant	Other Relevant	Stigma	Normal	Pair	Errors	Pair	Errors
Oralists								
Recruiters (R)	–	+	–	+	R/A_o	1	As/S	1
Searchers (S)	–	+	+	–	R/X	2	F/R	1
Aloofs (A_o)	–	–	–	+	A_o/S	3	F/A_o	2
							C/S	2
							C/A_o	3
							As/R	3
Signers								
Friends (F)	+	+	–	+	C/As	1	F/S	3
All they can do (As)	+	+	+	–	F/As	2	As/A_o	4
Changers (C)	+	–	+	–	F/C	3	C/R	4

are now directed at helping hearing-impaired children. Sally coordinates a mothers' group that tries to contact mothers of recently diagnosed deaf children, to comfort and to advise. Bob works with the fathers, but they never seem to have much time for meeting. Janie, their six-year-old deaf daughter, adorns the cover of the pamphlet soliciting contributions to the local speech-and-hearing association. Her speech is coming along fine. She has good tonal quality and knows a "few" signs.

Recruiters proselytize and advocate. They join, organize, and set up programs. They lecture and often write to provide "helpful" information to parents with recently diagnosed nonhearing children. They support organizations that promote oralism. Usually mothers, they are often enthusiastic and more than willing to give advice. Their children may be put on display to demonstrate what can be accomplished. "Janie, tell the lady where we went yesterday." Janie's verbal reply: "We went to the zoo." Everybody: "Isn't that amazing!" The essential characteristic of the recruiter is the evangelistic attitude that something must be done; he or she is an activist par excellence.

The recruiters' activity stems from their oralist stance. Hence, they advocate ordinary, everyday knowledge that is based on the presumption of hearing in an arena in which, prima facie, it does not belong. Like all oralists they do not recognize the special status of the deaf experience or its relevance to their own problems. There is irony here in that when oralists like Bob and Sally talk—as they do, long and often—about the special nature of their child and others like her, they mean not that such children are different but, rather, that they require more and individually tailored help to become like other children. When Bob and Sally discuss Janie's potential, they project the future on the basis of her acquisition of like-normal speech skills. Acquiring "normal" speech; changing popular attitudes toward hearing aids; and promoting positive, mainstreamed experience for hearing-impaired children are techniques for normalizing the experience of not hearing.

Standards of normality have supporting social frameworks. The recruiters proclaim that a child's lack of hearing is really insignificant when seen from the proper perspective. However, the framework of support for normality assumes hearing.[4] Thus the recruiter must show that remedial steps are available that will serve in the place of hearing. Work on speech training, manners, and dress, as well as special tutoring in academic subjects, will provide the opportunity for the child to "pass" as a hearing person. Acting on such logic, the recruiter moves into the parents' world of disappointment and shores up that world by attempting to point to its foundation.

The Searchers

Milt's job at the plant keeps him busy, with lots of overtime in the heavy season. In the off season, there's the bowling team and softball.

Peggy also has a job, as an inventory clerk for a parts company. Sometimes she has to work late. They make ends meet. When their daughter, Betty, was three years old and still not talking, they went to the doctor, who said they ought to have Betty's ears tested and told them about a local clinic. They received some advice and some suggestions about early education and options in education, teaching Betty to speak and to communicate, and the need for further testing. Peggy was confused; Milt was angry. They found out about another doctor, a specialist. He was supportive, explaining that surgery might be possible if the tests indicated it; but after several more visits, he said it was "nerve deafness" and there was "nothing he could do." Now Milt and Peggy are saving for a trip to the Central Institute, and Peggy has heard about a faith healer coming to town.

Compared with the two other types of oralists, searchers do not resign themselves to the difficult work of normalizing not hearing, that is, coming to grips with the problem. They are oralists, however, because they share with the others the presuppositions of the primacy of speech and the irrelevance of signs to one's personal identity. The searchers' response to the information that their child cannot hear differs from that of the other subtypes. They expend their energies, moving from one doctor to another, trying acupuncture, visiting faith healers if they are so inclined, and utilizing other extramedical remedies. In a way, seachers manifest a degree of authenticity not found among other oralists, in that they are honestly and straightforwardly attempting to restore "hearing." They cannot accept what they know to be true, namely, that the absence of hearing means a different way of life. Their search for a cure is an admission of the stigma associated with deafness. The other types of oralists have accommodated their common-sense version of the nature of the social world to the knowledge that their child cannot hear. Accommodation does not change the infrastructure of knowledge.[5] This is accomplished by applying meanings of work in a way that renders not hearing insignificant to "life experiences."

In short, oralism nullifies deafness as a cultural entity. Searchers have not yet achieved a degree of competence that allows the nullification to occur; that is, they have not yet reached the "proper" understanding of not hearing. Although they will not accept a new alternative structure, one that allows the social dimensions of deafness, they have not yet advanced to the *nonrecognition* of deafness. They feel that not hearing must mean more than "special education" and "personality adjustments." It is this tacit recognition of the deaf world that keeps Milt and Peggy searching.

Searching is difficult to sustain and usually represents a transition to one of the other subtypes of oralism. However, since the differences among the subtypes are largely a matter of emphasis, a parent may move freely and simultaneously among the three subtypes. For instance, a parent may cautiously entertain acupuncture while confidently purchasing the newest, most-powerful and least-obtrusive hearing aid. The nature of the discovery of not hearing, the context of medical treatment, and the expectation of a cure all predispose most oralists to be searchers first, aloof and recruiters second (see Meadow, 1968). Searching is painful for the oralist because it comes close to the recognition of the social dimension of deafness. But in coming close to this recognition, in a brush with the untowardness of deafness, the oralists find new strength and rejuvenated power in their efforts to hold at bay "the deafs." It is almost as if oralism requires a frontier of searching, a way to rekindle the underlying hope that "really, our child is not different."

The Aloof

> Bill is a lawyer. He works for a corporation and is very successful. His wife is a graduate of an Eastern women's college. They travel, enjoy entertaining, and reside in a fashionable section of town. When their first-born child, Tina, was discovered to have a profound hearing loss, they were devastated. The child was to have followed in her parents' footsteps. Now what can be done? They have a close friend who is a physician. He refers them to a friend who knows about a good private school that specializes in handling these kinds of problems. The school is out of town and expensive but has a fine reputation. Many of its graduates speak and do quite well. They will tell Bill and his wife what to do, and Bill and his wife will listen.

Aloof oralists have little to do with organizations, other parents, or the networks of consultation that often develop among parents of the deaf. They work on their own, using correspondence courses and books until their child is old enough to attend an "oral" school or be boarded at an oral residential school. This entrustment of the child's education occurs at an exceptionally early age (sometimes as early as one year) and at the encouragement of educators. The authorities or experts, depending on their credentials and reputation, are regarded as invaluable in their judgment of the superiority and desirability of a talking child over a signing one. Aloof oralists do not focus their lives around the child in a direct fashion. They prefer a quiet, well-mannered child. Bill and his wife will seek out the school that is best for their child and best for them. They will not change their interpretation of the pathological nature of not hearing, and they will go to great extremes and expense to preserve their own way of life. Their adaptation to their child's condition is to reject any mode of visual communication for themselves. They regard such systems as untoward and capable of stigmatizing both themselves and their child. They are often totally indifferent toward the deaf community. Even if they are aware of the world of the deaf, they do not see that world as relevant to their problem. Visual communication would draw attention to their child and force them to work out some personally acceptable reasons for being different from ordinary people. Deaf people and their activities simply have nothing to do with the kind of help Tina requires. These parents are not aggressive, and they develop and employ many normalization techniques in dealing with their children. Chief among these is the "special school."

Characteristics of Signing Types

If holding at bay the admission of the separate and distinctive nature of the phenomenon of deafness is the keystone of oralism, then the acceptance of that phenomenon is the hallmark of the signer. The signer begins from an acknowledgment, sometimes tacit and at other times calculated, of the social dimensions of deafness. *Not hearing* is taken to mean other sets of experiences, other ways of interpreting, "otherness," "outsider and insider perspectives," and "separateness." In some cases, such recognition is accompanied with an evaluation. Thus the signer may consider the deaf experience to be not only different but also less desirable, one that carries a stigma.

Signing by a hearing person in a public place draws the same stares, the same curiosity and mockery that the deaf know so intimately (Higgins 1980b). Of course, the hearing may switch codes and use spoken English to leave behind the deaf identity. Nevertheless, the experience and the separateness are felt. Simply deciding to sign is sufficient to broaden a person's horizons. First, the decision presupposes that signs are teachable, not merely an incoherent set of gestures but, rather, a developed system of communication. Further, the acknowledgment of signs brings the acknowledgment of the possibility of the deaf experience itself. Thus, in much the same way that even unsuccessful sojourns into learning a second, third, and fourth language provide opportunities for expanded consciousness, so knowing and using signs likewise opens the door to knowing what it means to be deaf.

The acknowledgment of signs, however, involves "mixing styles," putting incompatible qualities together. To know about an "aberrant" type in any detail requires the management of information so as to avoid acquiring the aberrant identity; and the putative equality of the deaf experience is difficult to maintain in the face of broader societal horizons. One should learn only "approved," highly developed languages and, incidentally, those with little threat to general society; hence, the decision to learn a low-status language is in itself an act of consciousness expansion, one consequence of which may be a weakening of the common-sense structure of ordinary knowledge.

The signer is not rebellious in an ordinary sense. She may be conservative, hard working, and very religious. In fact, fundamentalist, working-class backgrounds provide a supporting base that is conducive to the acceptance of signs. Working- or lower-class parents, by virtue of their own low status, have developed friendships, work relationships, and social activities that characteristically lie outside the mainstream of middle-class society. No doubt, there are many presuppositions or precepts of cultural life that cut across lines, such as the Western world's view of the duality of thought (the tendency to think in terms of opposites) or the assertiveness of humans over nature. However, these cultural precepts manifest themselves in different ways at different class levels. Among the lower classes, assertiveness may be more obtrusive. Working-class persons have a sense of immediacy and an awareness of their low status that in some produces a compulsion to move up but, more often, creates a milieu of contemporaneity composed of varied biographical derivations. As sociologists have long noted, those who are down and out, who inhabit "the other worlds of the social outcast," are complex beyond one's initial impression. Within this milieu, owing to the closeness and daily contact with many kinds of persons, signs are accepted as a part of "our world." The acceptance of signs assumes one of several modes of adaptation.

The Handicapped or All-They-Can-Do Type

> Al has had three different jobs in the last few years. He is a high-school graduate with minimal skills. He can operate a fork lift and light equipment. He usually finds work in warehouses, work that is not steady. Evelyn, Al's wife, is a waitress. She does not earn much, but her job at the pancake house provides some security and support. The women at the restaurant are a tightly knit group. Al and Evelyn have known bad times. They lost their house a few years ago when they could not make the payments, and they now live in a small apartment with their three children. Donny, the second born, is deaf. Although the news was a shock, and it took a while to get used to it, Al had worked with a deaf man, and Evelyn saw deaf people having breakfast before church just about every Sunday. Her church even provides an interpreter for Sunday services. She always considered talking with one's hands a fascinating thing. Although they have had neither the time nor the skill to learn much sign, they can tell what Donny wants; and his education is "taken care of."

One adapatation to deafness involves the "all-they-can-do" attitude. The attitude does not ordinarily entail condescension toward the use of sign as much as an acquiescence to the low esteem that sign has in the society. The deaf child is not so much rejected or denied as he or she is placed within a perspective that is class bound and, secondarily, sign bound. This type of signer may be content to know just enough sign to handle family affairs pertaining to the management of the child's behavior and to acknowledge that the deaf world is "out there" and stigmatized. The child is located in that barely known world, and his or her employment aspirations and support for training are ordered accordingly. "All he can do" is be a deaf carpenter, a deaf plumber, a deaf printer, or, if a girl, a keypunch operator, seamstress, and so on. After all, that is the type of work the parents do. In Al's case, there is even the possibility that Donny will do better than his parents. Such an adaptation is an extension of a more-general adaptation to class location with the added dimension of deafness, which is likewise understood in class terms. As Al remarked, "Sure, we know bad times, but so does everybody else. That's the way the world is. You have to live in it as you find it." He continued, "I don't know many deafs, but I seen 'em work; they're damn good workers, and they look like they're doin' okay to me." Among the working-class people there is a feeling of consciousness of class identity. Often this feeling may be vague, and in a few cases it may be the basis for prejudice. For example, if the life-style of a group held in low esteem is acknowledged and accepted by members of another group, then the implication is that the two groups are similar in life-style. However, when people regard others whose backgrounds are similar as having "made it," as "doin' okay," or as "keeping their heads above water," they place less stress on how this was accomplished than on the results of the accomplishment. If the deaf world exists and people in it are "doin' okay," then it is the results that count.

The Sign Changers

> Gary and Margaret both finished college with the feeling that they should do something meaningful. In college they were in service organizations and did volunteer work with underprivileged children. Gary once thought about joining the Peace Corps but married Margaret instead. He worked for a while with the city government before going back to graduate school. After working his way through school, he finally landed an administrative job at a junior college. He still had work to do on his degree, which he finished last year after three years of part-time effort. Margaret is a devoted mother. Her first born, Amy, is deaf. Margaret and Gary organized a parent group to pressure the public-school system into offering a total-communication class. Gary's position with the junior college helped their cause. Margaret is concerned about quality early education for all children. She volunteers at the open school just in order to keep up on new developments since she left college. They know that Amy's language must be visual, but they also feel that it must be "correct."

Usually more highly educated than the all-they-can-do type and usually middle-class themselves, the sign changers have arrived at a recognition of signs not simply as a given but also as the result of exploration. This exploration may be of the deaf world itself through acquaintance with deaf relatives, neighbors, or friends of the deaf; or it may have come from a journey through the "miseducation" of deaf children (Cicourel and Boese 1972). Sign changers are frequently converts from oralism. They are the devotees of "siglish." They use

signs in accordance with English syntax, inventing "signs" as direct counterparts to English words. Curiously, they correct their child's "language" in
much the way that hearing middle-class parents attempt to shape their children's speech into approved grammatical sentences. For example, Amy signs,
"put sticky tires on motorcycle, make motorcycle go good." The parent corrects "go well," fingerspelling *w-e-l-l*. Having been converted to a visual mode
of communication, sign changers become preoccupied, almost obsessed, with
the goodness of fit between signs and spoken English. In some respects, they
share the proselytizing attitude of the oralist recruiter; but their object is the
deaf experience itself or, more accurately, their interpretation of that experience. They know of the separateness of the deaf experience but wish to bring
it in line with the hearing world insofar as that is possible. Further, they believe
that this can be accomplished on a linguistic dimension, that is, by signing
proper English.

Sign changers at least know of the deaf experience. They often have deaf
adults as friends; some may even have visited deaf clubs and may carry on
correspondence with deafs. They know of, but are not necessarily part of, that
subcultural domain. They are marginal and on the fringes of deafness, a condition they readily demonstrate through their propensity to intervene in the deaf
world on behalf of the hearing world or to serve as representatives of the deaf
world. They may assist deaf persons by "correcting" their written English or
generally functioning as "friendly" symbols of the hearing world. However, they
are grounded in a hearing infrastructure and are merely venturing into the deaf
world for their child's benefit. It is not that sign changers are insincere or
malevolent; they are simply *primarily* hearing. The basic precepts and assumptions about the nature of social life are essentially the same for the sign changer
as for the oralist. The difference is in the acknowledgment of a deaf experience,
at least that part of it that is rooted in linguistics.

Sign changers have become aware that visual communication is necessary
for the deaf. However, the complete social character of sign is not fully appreciated or, at any rate, is assigned to a position of secondary relevance for assessing language adequacy among the deaf. In other words, sign changers are not
ordinarily interested in signs per se. They are not concerned with the broader
"horizons of meaning" associated with signs (Cicourel and Boese 1972). Their
interest is only in those aspects of sign language that are easily placed in an
English context or environment. Those aspects of signs that are distinct from
English are ignored or regarded as idiosyncratic and unimportant to the task
of achieving a "good fit." Sign changers are not interested in idiomatic sign
expressions, for instance.

The sign changer advocates such communication systems as "seeing exact
English," or "signed English" as part of total commication for education. Deaf
adults may accommodate these parvenus on the grounds that new signs are
"good for the children." Still, the sign changers' signing appears strange,

pedantic, and often incomprehensible to the deaf. Although some deaf teenagers and adults publicly acquiesce in and even sincerely approve "total communication" as an improvement over their own school experiences, many privately believe that children who have experienced total communication will return to the "old signs" or the "real signs" (ASL) as they become part of the deaf community. For example, despite systematic efforts to teach "new signs" to deaf adolescents, when these adolescents are chatting in friendship groups, either they do not use these signs at all or they incorporate them in ASL syntax. Some of these adolescents may be exposed to signed English as their first "visual language." Even so, they tend to use ASL among themselves and return to signed English only with hearing signers.[6] Recently, of course, many late adolescents have become increasingly militant about their rights to use ASL in any context they choose.

The sign changers are child oriented, middle class, and pedagogical. They are not hostile toward the deaf; they simply approach them with an air of superiority. Again, this is not the deliberate intention of the sign changers but is a consequence of their attitude toward the signs and their appraisal of the inadequacy of the signs for what they consider educational and cultural affairs. They accept that deaf children must acquire a language visually; but they feel that, since society is the way it is, the closer the visual scheme approximates English patterns, the better.

Perceptually, the thinking of sign changers may be portrayed as follows: Of course, we know you have your world and it's fine as it is; but if you want to make it in this world—and you must—then you need to adopt the approved form as your own. Such a mandate is impossible to achieve, but this precept is not designed for comparisons among different sets of experiences with any degree of objectivity. It already prejudges the superiority of one set. These signers do not think of the social world as multidimensional but, rather, assume that it is unmalleable and one dimensional.

The Friends of the Deaf

It was particularly ironic that Tom and Olivia's first child should be deaf. Tom grew up living next door to a deaf family. Tom was very friendly with the boys from that family, especially Luke, who was his age. They played together after school until high school separated them. Tom went to the local high school and on to college, while Luke went to the deaf school out of town and then worked as an electrician. Tom did not remember much about how they communicated. He had forgotten the signs he once knew. But his memory of that family was vivid, and he occasionally got a letter from Luke. Olivia knew nothing about deaf people; when their daughter was diagnosed as profoundly deaf, she was sure that the little girl's life was going to be abnormal. Together, Tom and Olivia began a process of rediscovering what Tom already knew. At first they followed the advice of the speech clinic, the John Tracy course, and the parent groups. Throughout these early days of hearing people talking about deafness and what to do, Tom kept remembering Luke. Tom also was beginning to meet some deaf people who served as liaison between the hearing organizations and the deaf community. Tom liked these people, and soon he and Olivia were being invited for dinner and were attending the deaf church. Members of the community cared for one another's children as much as possible. Tom and Olivia attended a church-sponsored sign-language class. They are not "like the natives" yet, but they are learning to listen to hands.

Friends of the deaf share with other types of signers their recognition of the deaf experience, but they participate in that experience to a much greater degree than do the other two subtypes. Occasionally, hearing parents do try to become friends of the deaf. However, the deaf often hold these parents at a distance, suspecting them to be sign changers or meddlers. There are, of course, rare circumstances in which a parent masters ASL, becomes adapted to the deaf world, and functions with dual membership. But observation reveals that this adaptation will occur only under some highly specific conditions. For example, signs must be used constantly within the context of the immediate family as well as when outsiders are present during visits with the family. Signs must not be an interpretive step between the deaf child and the hearing person but must be equal to speech or become the primary medium for conversing. Obviously, among hearing persons who have been socialized through a spoken language, such an effort requires perseverance and commitment. The presence of a deaf adult or a native signer is almost a prerequisite for the the elevation of signs to a primary level within a hearing family. The most-frequent adaptation among those who are motivated in this direction is to bring signs under English, that is, to introduce signed English or a pidgin tending toward the English end of the sign-English continuum.

Implications of Types

We have offered a characterization of each type in terms of a four-value scheme. Through case descriptions, we have attempted to describe the presumptive basis from which parents of each type operate. Typological analysis also allows for the derivation of relationships among the types according to purely formal criteria.

Each type is defined by a unique configuration of values. Only the dimension of regarding some type of signing system as relevant to the practical affairs of everyday life (self-relevant) distinguishes parents into two broad categories (oralists and signers). Hence, our typology generates comparisons on the three other dimensions for all the types. These comparisons reveal that attitudes toward signing systems alone do not adequately depict the social distances between types of parents. In fact, a match of configurations for each pair of types shows that some signers—friends and all-they-can-do types—are closer to some oralists (aloof and recruiter types) than they are to their fellow signers (changers). The greatest differences, as measured by mismatches in the paired comparisons (errors), and hence the greatest distance between types, occurs for recruiters and changers, and for aloof oralists and all-they-can-do signers.

The two values for manual communication may be thought of as a process in which a parent associates or dissociates with a potentially discrediting mode of communication. Obviously, a rejection of any manual system places distance between the parent and actual members of the deaf community. Still, in describing "distance" it is important to distinguish among the parents' attitudes toward the use of signs for others. Recruiters and searchers readily admit that such systems are useful for others. They differ in that recruiters normalize their offspring's not hearing by regarding it as qualitatively different from "being deaf." Searchers, on the other hand, stigmatize not hearing by avoiding the attribution of the stigma to themselves through failing to acknowledge fully that their child is really deaf. Aloof parents simply avoid attending to the problems of managing stigma by maintaining an interpretation of the meaning of not hearing that keeps any potential discrediting information away from them. In this fashion they can regard their offspring's problem as normal within the context of their knowledge of the special problems of parenting.

For signers we see similar patterns. Both friends and all-they-can-do types admit the relevance of signs for others, whereas changers do not. All-they-can-do types and changers stigmatize the deaf experience, whereas friends normalize it by recognizing the cultural dimensions of the deaf community. Although modes for normalizing differ for recruiters, aloofs, and friends (recruiters and aloofs stress mainstream values, whereas friends accent subcultural values), all these types attempt to avoid the stigma of deafness. Searchers, changers, and all-they-can-do types on the other hand, stigmatize deafness. Each type associates or dissociates according to a unique thought process.

By treating parents in terms of typological contrasts, we can understand that parents cannot be categorized nicely as signers or oralists. Further, we can see that depending on the issues in question, oralist and signing parents may find themselves in either closer accord or greater discord than may different types of either signing or oralist parents. For instance, on the issue of mainstreaming a child, recruiters and changers, prima facie, should be in agreement in principle, both favoring the policy. However, since they differ so dramatically in how they evaluate the deaf experience, stigmatizing it for others as opposed to normalizing for oneself, these parents may be at fundamental odds. Changers may be forced into strong justifications for visual-English programs (self-contained classes) that may be seen as a distinctive mode by hearing children and teachers, and recruiters may be nonplused by a policy of total integration since they downplay the visual mode in the first place. Hence, we can ascertain that the interpretive styles used by parents may play themselves out in distinctive practical consequences. In some instances signers may favor mainstream policy and ignore deaf-adult-community members, whereas in others oralist types may be willing to heed the advice of deaf-community members.

Conclusion

Parents can be classified into a typology, the dimensions of which are both linguistic and social. The acceptance of visual-communication systems is not the same as knowing of, appreciating, or participating in the deaf experience. As the typology illustrates, some forms of adaptation to having a deaf child involve visual communication but rejection of the deaf experience, whereas some parents who do not sign nevertheless seem to acknowledge the existence of a deaf experience. It is important to note in conclusion that the deaf experience is largely outside the parent's understanding. Parents care and hope for their children's well-being both in the present and in the future. They care and they hope in the only way they know, as hearing people. However, this means that they may never fully acknowledge the experience of being deaf as potentially complete in and of itself. Since their children are deaf, they deny them that completeness, at least as family members. These considerations may be clear to the sociological observer, but only parents can decide what they mean to their lives with their children.

Notes

1. The typology presented is based both on systematic observations of parents in various private and organizational settings and on personal experiences. The types are not statistical averages derived from observations but are constructed typifications of observations (McKinney 1970, pp. 244-248). The types are intended to sensitize the reader to values, goals, and ways of thinking that can be discovered among parents of deaf children. The cases are fictitious, but they are composite portrayals of actual life situations.

2. This presumption is a necessary condition for social interaction. In order to interact, participants must assume that for the purposes at hand they have identical mental points of view. They must further assume of each other that these viewpoints are interchangeable. This assumption goes unchallenged unless one of the parties calls it into question through what the other party regards as inappropriate thoughts, feelings, or actions. A recognition of this assumption illustrates the relative or contrived nature of social interaction.

Such an expansion of consciousness may threaten beliefs about what is taken for granted about the way the world is (Cicourel 1970, pp. 33-34; Schutz 1962, pp. 11-12).

3. This is a description of the meaning this kind of person imputes to situations that he recognizes as ranked. We are discussing people's common-sense knowledge. These people can be characterized on the basis of the manner in which they have made sense out of their past experiences. Thus they "know" that to be successful, one must look successful; one must not rock the boat; one wins by playing the game better than anyone else; one plays by the rules; and so on (see Cicourel's 1970 discussion of status and role as negotiations).

4. McHugh (1970) has suggested that the judgment of an act as "not normal" is based on two assumptions: that the person had alternatives for action and that he knew what he was doing. Recruiters' labeling of deafness as deviant presumes that the person has alternatives to not hearing, namely, passing as a hearing person. Their understanding of not hearing operates on the rule, "Might it have been otherwise?" This rule has built into it a judgment of deviance. Recruiters, therefore, not only fail to understand deafness but also, by virtue of their way of thinking, close off the possibility of understanding (see McHugh 1970, pp. 178-179).

5. Infrastructure refers to the subconscious or subtheoretical values, assumptions, and goals that support the oralist mentality. The level is one of presuppositions that are shaped by the larger culture (see Gouldner 1970, pp. 46-49).

6. One of the problems these teenagers often face is that signed English requires total communication; that is, it is usually not possible to understand signed English without simultaneous lip movements. Although the ASL they produce is awkward at first and they have difficulty "reading" deaf friends who are signing without lip movements in ASL syntax, these barriers usually disappear rapidly for them.

6

How the Deaf See the Hearing

In this chapter, an ethnography of the deaf community describes the role conceptions that the deaf have of hearing people. These conceptions can be ranked in terms of how the deaf perceive equivalence between themselves and the hearing. Type I conceptions connote the most equivalency; type II conceptions refer to hearing persons who know of and use some form of manual communication; type III conceptions represent the greatest perceived distance from membership in the deaf community. The implications of the use of these conceptions in communicative exchanges are derived.

Complex society is composed of many cultural domains (Spradley 1972). In communicating across these domains, people do not necessarily accomplish accurate conceptions of one another (Habermas 1970; Sherohman 1977). Rather, they construct entire images of types of others and then use these images to judge relationships they might have with people they take to represent a particular type (Schutz 1962; Lyman and Scott 1970).

For a given instance of communication across domains, or cross-modal communication (Cicourel 1974a), a full understanding of this exchange depends on the analyst possessing documentation of the role conceptions that serve the interactants as backgrounded features (Cook-Gumperz 1975, pp. 138-139). As Cicourel (1974a, pp. 165-171) demonstrates in his treatment of exchanges between himself and a deaf woman, such situations are not indicative of a "language problem" alone, that is, a matter of simple translation. Instead, they embody whole systems of backgrounded interpretations and sense-making procedures. The explication of these backgrounded features seem to be a crucial step toward an understanding of deaf-hearing interchanges. The present chapter offers an ethnographic description of the role conceptions the deaf have with regard to the hearing.

Deaf-Hearing Exchanges as Cross-Modal Communication

Deaf people's conceptions of hearing people represent distinctive *backgrounded features* that the deaf owe to their membership in the deaf community. Reliance

This chapter is a revised and expanded version of Jeffrey Nash and Anedith Nash, "Distorted Communicative Situations as a Function of Role Conceptions in Deaf–Hearing Communication," *Sign Language Studies* (Fall 1978):219–250. Used with permission of Linstok Press.

on a visual means of communication and the minority status of such communication have provided a grounding among the deaf for a "consciousness of kind." Shared community experiences function as scenic background for communicative exchanges and are embodied within the signs.[1]

The signing community can function as a kind of refuge from the hearing society in which associations the deaf re₁ᵣd as natural can be constructed and maintained. The deaf live daily in contac t with hearing people; however, they achieve intersubjective meanings through their interactions with other deaf, signing people. It is their symbolic contacts with hearing people and the significance of these impinging influences on the meanings and experiential horizons of the deaf (Cicourel and Boese 1972) that forms the focus of this analysis.

Through interviews with deaf adult informants in two Midwestern cities and from observations gathered at deaf community functions we compiled information sufficient to allow us to do a componential analysis of the way deaf people perceive the hearing. Our analysis led to fine distinctions, paring these perceptions down to basic semantic features. These parings resulted in composite information presented in table 6-1.

The analysis revealed that conceptions of roles that hearing people assume can be classified and subdivided. Table 6-1 rank orders the conceptions according to the deaf persons' imputed equivalence with the hearing. Thus, children of the deaf (a categorization that applies regardless of age) are regarded as "closest to one of us." These are people whose parents were deaf and who presumably acquired a native-language competency in signs in the home in much the same manner as if they themselves had been deaf. At the other extreme, professionals received imputed characteristics distancing them from the deaf community and, hence, highlighting incongruent backgrounded features.

The analysis of the features of role conceptions allows for the identification of three broad types: type I, the almost deaf; type II, the mostly hearing; and type III, the completely hearing.[2] Selected role conceptions for each type will be discussed in order to relate the patterns of meaning for the configurations as a whole.

Type I Conceptions: The Almost Deaf

This type comprises two role conceptions: children of the deaf and interpreters. Both conceptions rest on assumptions of high degrees of competence in manual communication. The children of the deaf generally are regarded as more likely to be comfortable with ASL, whereas interpreters may have greater competence in English. Hence, the interpreter may be expected to represent the hearing world to a greater degree than would the children of the deaf.

Children of the deaf may choose either deafness or hearing, depending on motivation and intent. At times they may be attuned to the deaf experience

Table 6-1
Taxonomy of Role Conceptions

| Hearing People | Manual Communication | | | Intercession | | Interest in Interaction | | Motives | | Types |
	Native Signer	Finger Spelling	Signed English	Provide	Require	Intrinsic	Extrinsic	Trustworthy	Suspicious	
1. Children of the deaf	Yes	Yes	Yes	Yes	No	Yes	No	Yes	Yes	
2. Interpreters	Some	Yes	Yes	Yes	No	Yes	Yes	Yes	Yes	I
3. Siblings	Rarely	Some	Some	Yes	Yes	Yes	No	Yes	No	
4. Neighbors	No	Some	Some	Yes	Yes	Yes	Yes	Yes	No	
5. Coworkers	No	Some	Some	Yes	Yes	Yes	Yes	Yes	Yes	II
6. Parents of deaf children	No	Some	Some	Yes	Yes	No	Yes	No	Yes	
7. Educators	No	Some	Some	Yes	Yes	No	Yes	No	Yes	
8. Church people	No	No	No	No	Yes	No	Yes	Yes	No	
9. Oral, hearing imparied	No	No	No	No	Yes	No	Yes	No	Yes	
10. Organized helpers	No	No	No	No	Yes	No	Yes	No	Yes	III
11. Professionals	No	No	No	No	Yes	No	Yes	No	Yes	

Components of Meaning as Imputed Interactional Competency

and may be partially accepted as community members. At other times, they may move in the direction of the hearing to the exclusion of the deaf. In the company of both deaf and hearing persons, children of the deaf may opt for the hearing by speaking without simultaneously signing when conversing with other speaking people, thereby excluding the deaf persons present from full participation in the conversation. To the deaf it seems that the children's over-riding motivation in this setting is to avoid association with the isolating features of membership in the deaf community.

As interpreter, the hearing person occupies a strategic position because neither the hearing nor the deaf party to the conversation can monitor the interpreter's translations for correctness of intent and mood; and since the interpreter may unwittingly identify with the hearing person who is carrying on the conversation, these interpreted conversations are rarely equivalent rendi-tions. Instead, they become condensations that utilize the backgrounded fea-tures of spoken English. Since English serves as the dominant language in these situations, it appears to the deaf that interpretations are designed so that the hearing can go on with their talking (compare the notion of cross-talk in Goff-man 1971, pp. 25-26; see also Nash 1976 for a detailed exposition of the dynamics of this phenomenon in the classroom).

Children of the deaf and interpreters are seen as both helpful and hindering. Having served as go-betweens, often from a very early age, they appear ambiva-lent toward their parents and other deaf people. This role conception implies biculturality. However, in such persons' relationships with the hearing, the hear-ing aspects that function as scenic background are often dominant.

Within the deaf domain, parent-child relationships or even friendships stem from presumed equivalence grounded in membership in the deaf community. Within cross-modal communication, where the child of the deaf serves as inter-preter, the hearing conversational partner occupies a superior position. The deaf see this as a consequence of the organization of the social setting itself. The interpreter has the power to manipulate the interchanges, to affect the outcome of interaction as well as its tone. What is "said" may be different from what is "signed"; and, of course, the deaf have no way to check the "reverse interpre-tation" (signs to English). From the vantage point of the hearing person, although the interpreter has similar license with the signs that are rendered into speech, there is little danger of manipulation since the hearing are rarely depen-dent on the deaf as the deaf are dependent on the hearing in cross-modal exchanges.

The deaf person may also attempt to use the interpreter. Because of the perceived closeness of the type, the interpreter may become associated with the deaf (Goffman 1963, pp. 19-31). Since the interpreter is "wise" in this sense, he or she may join the deaf in trying to procure preferential treatment in contacts with authorities such as employers or police. Or the person con-ceived as playing a type I role may become the target of the deaf person's attempt to avoid interaction with nonsigning hearing persons. The deaf may request favors such as trips to the store, as if interpretation were necessary in these situations. The type I person may believe that such intercession is not called for but may do it anyway out of a sense of understanding the problems of being deaf.

The extraordinary circumstance of having to rely on outsiders for routine matters of everyday life and conversation places the deaf person in a unique position. The deaf both depend on and, perhaps, exploit the type I role player. Hence, the deaf display ambiguity and suspicion toward this type of hearing person, although not as much as toward the other two role types.

Type II Conceptions: The Mostly Hearing

Persons of this type are characterized by increased distance from the deaf experience. Much less equivalency is imputed to them than to those subsumed under type I. Their manual-communication skills are minimal, rarely including competency in ASL, but perhaps including fingerspelling and some use of signs within an English syntax. Educators, for instance, may be fluent in signed English but may be regarded as interested in the deaf only for educationally relevant purposes, for example, discussing reading problems, troubles with an offspring's behavior in school, and so forth.

The deaf usually live in neighborhoods that are predominantly hearing. "Neighbor" as a role conception implies a degree of acquaintance; although this degree may not be intimate even among the hearing, neighborly activities between the deaf and the hearing do rest on some conception of hearing people. In this conception the deaf person recognizes the importance that the hearing person's cooperativeness plays in the accomplishment of a relationship. Neighbors swap tools, transport each other's children, and engage in casual greetings (Useem and Gibson 1960). The deaf, however, cautiously interpret the willingness of the hearing to consummate such relationships. The possibility for errors of judgment is vast; hence, our observations turned up few visual symbols of friendship-like exchanges of dinner invitations. Deaf households primarily entertain other deaf persons, not necessarily from their neighborhood.

Our informants report friendly relationships with their hearing neighbors, including such practices as that of an adjacent household serving as a message center for telephone calls for the deaf household.[3] The hearing household in effect becomes "servant" to the deaf, depending on the willingness and assertiveness of the hearing and deaf persons, respectively. Problems may arise if, for example, the deaf fear the hearing family will sense imposition and importunate intrusions. Or the hearing family may ignore requests and third-party inquiries to defend against increased associations with the deaf. Typically, members of the deaf family will attempt to offer "favors"—trading work, mowing lawns during vacation, or even minor household repairs. The deaf, however, are again limited in this arrangement by what they impute as an unwillingness on the part of the hearing to trust the deaf with child supervision or other areas of responsibility.

Despite these problems, patterns of neighborliness do emerge. Children— usually hearing children—of the deaf may provide the initial contact between families. What routinely happens is that wives of the households develop helping relationships with the deaf family. To the extent that these neighborly activities rest on the deaf conception of the hearing, there is the possibility that incongruently matched backgrounded features will complicate the relationships.

Coworkers illustrate another important type II conception. They often have the most-constant contact with the deaf, and they may represent a genuine link between the two worlds in an area of crucial concern to both—the job. A liaison with a hearing coworker can be extremely important to trouble-free employment for a deaf person. But to the deaf such liaisons seem difficult to accomplish.

The deaf think that the hearing feel that they are being burdened with extra work without recompense. They are aware that a deaf coworker is seen by the hearing as a job liability. However, our informants report that "communicative adjustments" are worked out in many cases. These are achieved in a variety of ways: through the use of writing (not the most-preferred method, according to the opinions expressed to us); through the use of speech and lip reading (although seemingly ideal for the hearing, very taxing and less than 100-percent efficient for both parties); or, most typically, through a mixture of several methods, including the acquisition of a fair-sized repertoire of signs on the part of the hearing. We observed that, in low-skill occupations (manual or maintenance work), a hearing coworker would be likely to learn some signs and fingerspelling as an adaptation to the deaf worker. The linguistic base between the two workers could become the groundwork for friendship relationships that might include even joke telling and practical joking. Components of the signs would be modified by both the hearing and the deaf, resulting in a code that is neither signs nor English (see Woodward 1973).

Still, such an occupational code reflects the cross-modal nature of the exchanges. For example, joke telling takes on two separate nuances each of which is sufficient reason for the telling. To the deaf, signing a joke can be an opportunity for self-expression and the display of acceptance. To the hearing, the telling of jokes becomes a way to "laugh at" the deaf person.

An old joke in signs goes like this. A deaf man was waiting in his car at a drawbridge with an attendant on duty. He waited and waited. Finally, impatient, he hurried from his car to the attendant's booth and wrote on a piece of paper "please 'but' the bridge." (The sign for *but* is made with the index fingers of both hands crossed. The hands are moved in opposite directions in an upward movement.) This joke could be funny to the hearing coworker because it is nonsense in English, a reflection of the deaf person's strange use of the language. Likewise, a joke told in "broken" signs by the hearing could be a source of humor to the deaf because of the way in which the signs are misused. As long as neither party to the exchange recognizes the incongruent backgrounded features, the relationship balances precariously on a misunderstanding.

The coworker may well be willing to admit the deaf into the world of work, but, as is true of coworkers in general, such admission does not necessarily imply friendship of an intimate nature. Hence, the deaf report wishing to avoid embarrassing a coworker by showing up unexpectedly at the door of his home. The potential for embarrassment seems to derive from the deaf person's conception of the hearing person. The hearing coworker would be embarrassed by the deaf person outside of the world of the job. The judgment of possible embarrassment stems from a suspension on the part of the deaf of the presumption that hearing is necessary for interaction, a presumption that is part of the backgrounded features for interaction available to the "ordinary" person. In other words, a deaf person is a display that other grounds for interaction are possible. The advent of such a person calls into question some presumptions of ordinary interaction. Hence, the hearing person must account for the presence of the deaf person: "Oh, I work with him down at the plant." Needless to say, deaf persons report wanting to avoid such encounters and tend to limit social contact with the hearing to the work scene itself.

Within the role conception "parents of deaf children" there is a sharp subdivision between those who use signs and those who are "oral," that is, insist on the exclusive use of lipreading and speech for communicative competency. Here we focus not so much on the properties of educational philosophy as on how that philosophy makes the parents appear to the deaf.

There is no lexical item in ASL denoting "oralism" or "total communication." New signs are often introduced for the specific purposes of updating ASL; but from the deaf perspective the salient consideration is the sign as a backgrounded feature. Hence, the invented sign for *total communication* uses a *t* and *c* hand shape within the basic two-handed sign for *conversing*. This represents a violation of ASL phonology, which requires that in signs involving two-handed movements the shape of the hands must be the same.[4] Hence, the enthusiasm with which the hearing tamper with the language of the deaf provokes both suspicion and amusement toward the hearing person.

Of course, what parents see as their child's problem (not hearing) is simply a taken-for-granted condition for deaf-community members. Further, the deaf suspect that the primary concern of the parent is that their children not become "like deaf people." The parents, if they sign at all, are more than willing to sign in English syntax without regard for violations of the linguistic rules of the signs. Although the deaf may be grateful to the parents for their initial recognition of the use of hands in communication, closer contacts with the parents often reveal that they are not genuinely and authentically interested in either signs or the deaf community.

Parents who employ manual forms of communication involving some elements of sign are, indeed, closer to the deaf in terms of role conceptions than are those parents who eschew all manualism. Still, parents rarely learn to use signs well enough to function as a liaison between the hearing and deaf worlds.

A common pattern does emerge for prolonged exchanges between the deaf and parents with deaf children. The deaf, generally with reluctance, may try to gain the services of such parents for routine affairs such as maintaining friendships among their children. Also, from the deaf viewpoint, acquaintance with such people may have a social value. For example, when entertaining a teacher from his former residential school, one deaf man invited his hearing "friends" to dinner with his family and teacher, apparently in order to demonstrate to this teacher his success in the hearing world. Parents of deaf children are of value in this capacity precisely because they have *not* acquired dual membership in both worlds. Thus they can be displayed as hearing people. The display is intended to say, "See, if they just give a little, we can get along well; and these people have done just that. Here they are in my home eating with us."

"Educators" include hearing teachers of the deaf, principals, administrators, and special educators of all varieties. What all of these have in common is that they are very rarely, if ever, signers of ASL. In most training programs for deaf education, the maximum exposure to manual communication of any kind is one semester or one course, with the election of an advanced course if such opportunities are available. Thus the deaf-education major will have only minimal acquaintance with the signs as the deaf use them.

Others in the educational system that impinges on the deaf experience will have only passing familiarity with signs or with deafness from the perspective of the deaf. This point can be illustrated by contrasting the meaning of lipreading to educators with its meaning to the deaf. To the deaf, lipreading is a highly taxing and tedious activity for even short periods of time. Since the deaf person does not have the same knowledge of the backgrounded features of English that the native hearing speaker has, even an excellent deaf lipreader can function at peak efficiency only within contexts where the speaker is known, the topic is not shifted often, and the number of speakers is limited.

However, a high-level administrator, head of special education in the public-school system of a large midwestern city, remarked in an interview that he had read that FBI agents could be taught to lipread very efficiently even when viewing a speaker from as far away as fifty feet. So, he continued, he did not understand why teachers could not do better with deaf children. Naturally, the comparison between native speakers concerned with one-way comprehension only and prelingually deaf children attempting the reading of sounds never heard from a language not known reflects ignorance of the deaf perspective.

Educators seem most often preoccupied with the question of integrating deaf persons into the hearing world. To the deaf, integration appears to "become the same as or equivalent to the hearing." However, to the deaf this matter has already been settled. The meanings of their everyday lives are embodied in the signs. They are concerned about practical matters—how to shop for the best buys; how to enter into fair credit and other business arrangements with adequate understanding of the terms of the contract; and how to avoid discrimination in areas such as service, jobs, and fringe benefits. The deaf do not see these problem areas as simple "translations" from their language to English. To them, efforts at integration have a misleading aspect. Such programs, they believe, obscure the realization that the differences between deaf and hearing people are social and cultural as well as physical.

Type III Conceptions: The Completely Hearing

Here four kinds of roles can be described: those of church people, oral hearing impaired, organized helpers, and professionals. All of these are regarded as having no communicative competency, requiring an intercessor from a person of type I or II, and interested in the deaf for extrinsic reasons only. People to whom such roles are imputed are suspiciously judged, except in the case of church people, whose motives are considered partially trustworthy because of their affiliation with a church that serves the deaf. The deaf role conceptions of these hearing people highlight the incongruity of backgrounded features and make the possibility of assessing interactional consequences remote.

The oral hearing-impaired person has been reared in a hearing family and attended oral schools. He or she often is married to a hearing spouse and often has hearing children. These people cannot and will not sign. They are anathema to the deaf. They cannot hear, but they apparently are "hearing" in attitude and behavior. Because our focus is on imputed components of roles, we do not entertain questions of what these people actually are like. To the deaf, they are functionally equivalent to hearing persons. They cannot sign, have no membership in the deaf community, do not articulate deaf interests, and presumably are motivated by a desire to avoid contacts of any kind with the deaf.

The church has been a place for the deaf community to flourish. Often, the deaf attend the hearing churches; it is this situation to which the following remarks most clearly apply. Where churches for the deaf exist, the discussion applies to those hearing persons who participate in the deaf church. The deaf Sunday-school class in the hearing church is an extension of the community of the deaf in general. There is often a ranking of Sunday-school-class membership in terms of status within the deaf community—the Methodist over the Baptist, the Baptist over the Church of Christ, and so on. However, these rankings are not absolute since family ties between the deaf person and his parents may affect denominational affiliation. Nevertheless, the hearing church does play an active part in the deaf experience. Within the environment of the church lurk the "church people," hearing people who, for one reason or another, have an interest in the deaf. They visit the deaf Sunday School, help in organizing affairs, and serve as an official link between the deaf and hearing main-line organization. These people are typically nonsigners, require intercession, have interests not directly relevant to the deaf community, and are merely politely tolerated by the deaf.

The overlapping and interpenetrating character of role conceptions is illustrated with the example of the *religious signer*. Such people usually have an evangelical attitude toward the deaf and in some cases may actually be ministers. There are very few deaf ministers; hence, the religious signers deliver lectures and Bible lessons in signs and serve in the capacity of ministers to the deaf. They may even be "friends of the deaf," that is, interpreters or sometimes children of the deaf. They may be properly considered *interpreters* within a religious context. Religious signers probably are regarded as the least meddlesome of all hearing people insofar as the nature of the signs themselves are concerned. In their religious zeal, they are anxious to communicate to the deaf persuasively and understandably. To modify the signs in order to align signs with English would only impede contact with "lost souls"; therefore, the signs are used as much as possible as they are found, that is, as used by the local deaf community.

A strong assessment of the relationship between deafness and organized helpers is that, in the eyes of the deaf, helpers are among the farthest from any genuine understanding of deafness. Organized helpers as a type may be illustrated by those who hold membership in local associations that variously purport to promote speech and hearing. Most cities in America have such associations (*American Annals of the Deaf* periodically publishes a complete directory of these associations). Many of these associations are funded by some type of community-based financial support, with the ostensible goal of serving the deaf and the hard of hearing in the community. From the perspective of the deaf, speech-and-hearing associations and their boards of directors are composed of representatives of each of the types of hearing people. However, the *board* usually has a special connotation, signifying that organizational arrangements exist to accommodate the needs of the hearing—usually financial and social— with regard to the deaf. To be a board member, one must have at least acquiesced in the notion that responsibility to an association will be assumed on the presumption that the good of the organization coincides with the good of the people whom the association serves.

The functions of the board are often defined to subsume many different kinds of activities, for example, aid to students of deaf education (these are invariably hearing students), some assistance in the procuring of hearing aids for the needy, or payment of professional fees for diagnostic services (a way in which the organization actually subsidizes or underwrites the legitimacy of the professionals' role and responsibility toward the deaf).

Such a broad definition of the function of the association has the effect of making the board appear to the deaf as if its chief purpose is to serve the hearing who are interested in deafness. Thus, educational programs sponsored by the board are, more often than not, presented *by* the hearing *to* the hearing *about* the deaf, without the benefit of written scripts and sometimes with little concern for such important matters as visual contact whenever an interpreter is present.

A dramatic case in point comes from an observation made at an annual Christmas party for hearing-impaired children. This party is usually organized around several group leaders for the children's activities. These leaders are students from special-education programs for the deaf from a nearby university. These student leaders are sometimes nonsigners. Some of the children are from oral programs and cannot sign or, for that matter, would be considered "contaminated" if exposed to signs. Often the children at the party have hearing siblings, which means that the party games are invariably "hearing oriented." Further, instructions for the games are given in speech, and the process of the games is monitored through speech. As the deaf children stand and watch their hearing brothers and sisters go through the motions of the games, they sign to each other about matters unrelated to the games on the floor or ridicule these activities without fear of discovery.

On one occasion, a major group activity at the party was the singing of Christmas carols without accompanying signs. This state of affairs took place despite the song leader's own competency with signs. When questioned afterwards about why he did not sign, he replied that he had thought of it but did not want to offend anyone. It is no surprise that few deaf people, other than the children with hearing parents, regularly participate in the affairs of the association.

In one particular association, the deaf did participate, but usually through the committee for deaf adults, which meant separate memberships and activities—in effect an organization within an organization. The activities that they sponsored were mainly parties and subtitled movies. The association customarily did not aid in the defrayment of the cost. In effect, for all practical purposes, the deaf were not a part of the association or could be thought of as a sub-association within the association, having only official, nominal connections with the board itself.

Professional people surround themselves with an aura that is both impenetrable and attractive to the deaf. On the one hand, they represent hope for some new breakthrough; on the other hand, past experience reveals that they are aloof and often concerned with such small segments of the deaf person's biography that even minimal communication is impossible. Types of persons in the professional category include doctors; audiologists; hearing-aid dealers; and occasionally college-level teachers from special education, speech pathology, and related departments. These people are not, all in all, particularly valuable to the deaf; and the deaf often are not of primary interest to them. The deaf believe that they are merely objects of studies and experimentation, a source for fees, and so on.

Professional role conception may provide a reference point for some personal experience, for instance, a series of frustrating sessions with a speech therapist or a consultation with a psychiatrist whose therapy consists of having the deaf person *write* in English for hours at a time. However, these personal markers do not involve the professional *as* professional, that is, within his or her capacity as an expert. In other words, being a professional means one thing to those espousing an ethic and possessing expert knowledge and quite another thing to the deaf. The deaf usually will consult with professionals only as a last resort, or when the entrance of the professional into the life of a deaf person can be interpreted by other deaf people as evidence of the deaf person's willingness to cooperate and contact the hearing world. For example, the purchase of a new hearing aid can demonstrate willingness to venture into the world of the hearing professional.

Being deaf is the result of an acculturation process rooted in the presumption that not hearing is a permanent condition. The deaf live in a social world that has routine knowledge and meaning grounded in a four-sense existence. Professionals, on the other hand, view deafness as a pathology. The doctor, the lawyer, and to some extent the minister need not assume the deaf perspective. They are concerned with other matters defined by the aims and values of their respective professions: doctors, to cure; lawyers, to represent clients; and ministers to serve religiously understood needs. The deaf apparently sense this in their role conceptions.

Some professionals do establish rapport with the deaf. For instance, a deaf educator may be accepted as having dual membership in both the hearing and the deaf communities. However, it is important to recognize that an individual's professional standing is irrelevant to this process. The professional must display grounds other than professional expertise in order to win the confidence and trust of the deaf. He or she must demonstrate competence in the rudiments of the deaf experience itself, which, most importantly, means knowing the signs and using them as they are used by the members of the local deaf community. Only then can one's professional status be reinterpreted by the deaf as helpful for the purpose of mediating between the deaf and the hearing worlds. This is largely a matter of moving toward deaf conceptions of the hearing, at least for the purpose of interpretation.

In those rare cases where a professional becomes a "deaf," the professional eschews his expertise in favor of the role of servant or intercessor. This role is ordinarily characteristic of relationships with type I conceptions. In short, in such situations the role conception of the "professional" loses its salience in defining the total meaning of interactions.

Summary and Conclusion

In summary, three distinctive patterns or types may be ascertained from an array of ethnographically discovered role conceptions that the deaf have of hearing people. Type I is characterized by imputed competencies in manual communication and decreasing distance in role conceptualization. Type II constitutes an array of role meanings, perhaps best referred to as ambivalent. Some manual communication is presumed as well as mixed role-distancing attributes. Finally, type III represents the kinds of hearing roles most remote from the deaf and evokes the most suspicion, distrust, and anxiety at the prospect of actual interaction.

With regard to the choice of these backgrounded features in cross-modal communications, the following options are open to the deaf person:

1. He or she may disassociate from the deaf community and use what are believed to be the features that ground hearing exchanges. This entails acquiring native competence in spoken English and establishing intersubjectivity based on "accurate" role conceptions of the hearing.
2. He or she may employ conceptions grounded in the deaf experience for the purposes of guessing what the hearing are doing and what they really mean.

Both options result in communicative situations in which an understanding between the deaf and the hearing is difficult to establish. In the first instance, spoken English can only be a second language for the deaf, learned and used with signs (or some other "artificially contrived" system) as a native competency base (see Markowicz 1974). Of course, many deaf people lipread and pronounce English words well. However, the intersubjectivity that grounds their language usage must differ from that affecting the hearing person's use of the language. In short, spoken English for the purposes of social interaction does not mean the same thing to the deaf that it does to the hearing user.

In the second instance, the use of deaf conceptions not known to or used by the hearing sets up situations in which the hearing may be misunderstood. We have documented what we regard as typical meanings that often underlie deaf and hearing exchanges. Of course, these conceptions can change and may not be shared equally among members of the community. However, we offer these research results to indicate that such conceptions do exist and can be documented as a salient characteristic of "deaf" knowledge of the hearing.

Persons learning the language of the deaf and others wishing to communicate with the deaf may find it helpful in establishing rapport to take on the role of the deaf. In the absence of prolonged contact and intimate familiarity with the deaf, ethnographic descriptions can serve to forewarn researcher and practitioner alike.

Notes

1. Although varieties of sign language have been classified (Fant 1972; Stokoe 1980), these treatments of sign language stress a distinction between language systems developed and acquired as native among and in the presence of the deaf and modifications of sign language introduced by hearing people. Usually the modifications, known variously as siglish, sign English, Seeing Exact English, and so on, are introduced to the deaf after a native competency in sign language has been established or as a device for improving second (or first and only) language competency in English. These impositions on the signs do not constitute essentials of the deaf-community experience.

2. The phrases are English renditions of sign expressions. Signs translate literally, for type I, "like deaf"; for type II, "hearing"; and for type III, "really or true hearing."

3. Many deaf-community members have teletype adaptors (TTYs) for their phones, which enable them to communicate with others who also have this equipment. However, phone calls from people without TTYs must be monitored by a hearing person.

4. This example comes from a lecture delivered by William Stokoe during a seminar on sociobiology at the University of Minnesota in the winter of 1978.

7

Adaptations to Deafness: Action and Structure

In 1965 Sussman pointed out the promise of an application of general sociological theory to the understanding of deafness. His remarks went virtually unheeded. With hindsight his proposal seems premature, for two reasons. First, evoking theoretical conceptions in the absence of adequate empirical research about the everyday lives of deaf people could have lead to vacuous abstractions; second, the concepts he cited (marginality, deviancy and stigma, and family concepts) seemed to consist of a loosely articulated list of ideas. Without an explicit theoretical stance, researchers of deafness and sociologists whose work in other fields may be pertinent could not readily assess, first, the advantages of using sociological perspectives over more widely accepted hypotheses, or, second, the links between their seemingly unrelated research and the task of understanding deafness.

The cumulation of empirically grounded knowledge about the lives of deaf people and recent interpretations of the nature of structured social action make possible the task envisioned by Sussman. Since the seminal work of Stokoe (1978) on the linguistics of signs, a growing number of researchers have systematically studied the languages and communication skills of deaf people. This work, in turn, has spawned several sociolinguistic inquiries (Woodward 1972; Cicourel 1974a); concern with the social organization of deafness (Cicourel and Boese 1972; Higgins 1977, 1979a, b; Becker 1978) and a few attempts to apply interactionist conceptions of self-concept to the peculiar socialization of deaf children (Meadow 1969). This work, together with that of disciplines more conventionally focused on deafness (principally educational psychology), forms and impressive body of knowledge, which, when coupled with the increasingly sophisticated conceptions of the structure of social action (see Merton 1963; Goffman 1974; Stokes and Hewitt 1976; Gonos 1977; Dawes 1978) provides the apparatus necessary to address in formal terms the question of the social structures of deafness.

The Social Organization of Deafness

Early studies identified a process consisting of impaired communicative competency, educational disadvantages and resultant stigmatization leading to endogamy, class homogeneity, and a minority-group status (Lunde 1956; Vernon and Makowski 1969; Schein 1968; Schein and Delk 1974). The principal impetus for this process was typically located in the imputed and internalized stigma of deafness and of sign language itself (see Goffman 1963; Higgins 1977; Scott 1978). Such an emphasis documented the isolation of deaf people from mainstream society and implied adaptations that could be managed, given the disjunction resulting from communicative incompetence and the requirements for full participation in society. It is not surprising that the impact of this reasoning focused research and pedagogical concern on the management of information about the deaf person with respect to interaction with the hearing (see Moores 1978).

Certainly, the inability to speak and understand the speech of others represents a major problem. Researchers thus became interested in strategies for negotiating the stigma and group identities that often resulted from these endeavors (see Lofland 1976 for a discussion of management ploys and deception used in the accomplishment of interaction under discreditable conditions; and, more directly, Padden and Markowicz 1976; Higgins 1979b).

However, the theoretical treatment of societal reactions to deafness remains incomplete and less than formal. In the classic discussion of stigma, Goffman (1963) describes "discreditable" states so comprehensively that virtually everyone could experience—and, hence, attempt to manage—a "spoiled" identity. Recent analyses clearly highlight the constructed and malleable processes implicated in becoming "defected" (Garfinkel 1967; Lofland 1976). These conceptualizations, of course, emphasize general processes rather than attending to the distinctive character of a particular "defect." To this extent, a sociological appreciation of deafness seems attainable under, perhaps, the labeling approach (see Gove 1975).

But the peculiar character of deafness as a defect confounds the dynamics of stigmatization. Higgins (1977) writes that much of the character of deaf-hearing interactions derives from the degree to which *deafness as an impairment* disrupts the taken-for-granted assumptions of routine interaction. These impairments are presumed to be non-negotiable, and even deaf-deaf exchanges could reflect the internalized consequences of years of experience with distorted communicative situations. Further, ethnographies of the *distinctive features* of the social organization of the deaf community—that is, the normal or routine character of deaf-deaf exchanges—must be a part of a complete and formal theoretical statement.

Higgins (1977) stresses how the strategies that deaf people employ in their dealings with hearing people reflect less concern with their spoiled identities and more with the practical instrumentalities necessary for accomplishing the minimal requirements of social intercourse (see Cicourel 1974a on the nature of normal interaction). The means the deaf employ embody the nature of their impairment. For example, note writing may be misconstrued as a demand, as in handing a note to a bank teller; or a written message may be mistaken in a narrow sense, that is, not regarded as capable of being filled out or expanded.

Likewise, the speech production of the deaf lacks the self-monitoring devices of normal conversation; hence, its use is *intrinsically* strained and uncreative. Higgins corrects an "overstigmatized" conception of the deaf and implies an action perspective.

Those "accused" of a defect do have means toward achieving participation in society. Their identities as well as their participation with others of shared or dissimilar identities can be thought of as action (see Parsons 1937; Dawes 1978). Certainly, their means are uniquely conditioned by the nature of the impairment and the "constructed reality" of their everyday lives. The literature regarding the latter is rich. The existence of a viable "community of the deaf" is well documented (Higgins 1979a; Jacobs 1974; Schein 1968). That "consciousness of kind" derives from a shared language, common impairments, the resultant discrimination toward the bearers of those impairments, and specialized knowledge about the suffering and joy of a separate social identity.

Socioculturally, the community is complex. Its linguistic environment exhibits a unique diglossic situation (Stokoe 1970); a pidginization (Woodward 1972); and the presence of a natural language (Stokoe 1978; Woodward 1972; Klima and Bellugi 1979). The influence of English (see Battison 1978), negative attitudes toward the "natural language," and compensating mechanisms for the community's lack of geographical boundaries and for its weak institutional supports combine to make the deaf community a symbolic network of shared experiences and competencies that cuts across the identities of ethnicity; race (Becker 1978); and, to some extent, the class boundaries of society. The evidence is compelling that there exists, at least for those born deaf of deaf parents, a culture of deafness (see Spradley 1972). Entrance into this culture is often an "achieved status" for the deaf adult.

Toward a General Theory

A theory of adaptations to deafness must stress the means that those who share the impairment employ in order to participate in society. As Merton eloquently demonstrated, adaptations are often generated by a means-ends disjunction intrinsic to the organization of society. In this light, adaptations can be seen as *negotiated strategies* (Strauss 1978; Lofland 1976) for dealing with the salient problems of everyday life. A description of the resolutions of common problems leads the theorist to an identification of types (Merton 1963; McKinney 1970).

For the deaf, the problematic character of everyday life is accentuated and patterned by their impairment, by societal reactions to them, and by the sense they make from these reactions. Conversely, action that separates impairment-

related problems from those that derive from the "normal" character of interaction (Cicourel 1974a) exaggerate a deaf person's "consciousness of kind."

Patterned social action for the deaf may now be represented as resolutions
of a general means-end dilemma. The end is membership in society, and the
means consist of the use both of widely available strategies and of those uniquely grounded in the nature of the impairment itself.

Deaf Social Action

As Parsons (1937) conceived it, action is the result of voluntary choice made
within the constraints of culture and situation. Although there are several
interpretations of constraint and of the importance of "situated aspects" for
choice in theoretical literature (Tiryakian 1965; Goffman 1974; Stokes and
Hewitt 1976; Gonos 1977), recent treatments emphasize a dialectic between
preconstituted meanings (Schutz 1971) and the outcomes of "mutual interactive
work." Hence, the meanings or actions of everyday life unfold from a continuing
chain of interpretations and applications within interactive situations.

When action is patterned by strong disjunctive pressures intrinsic to the
organization or "frames of interaction" (Goffman 1974), it may be properly
described as an adaptation, that is, a modification of what is routine or normal,
a structured deviation (Merton 1963). A description of adaptations to deafness
will engage, first, the structural (cultural and situational) exigencies associated
with the impairment and, second, the resultant outcomes or negotiated patterns
of adaptive action.

Adaptation as a Function of Framed Interpretations

In Goffman's (1974) terms, an action may be said to be *framed* when its meanings are fixed and imposed by the organization of the wider society. The frame·
"owes its existence to the functioning of the whole" (Gonos 1977, p. 861).
A framed set of meanings are, then, given or preconstituted. They define the
boundaries within which patterned choices may occur. They function to render
understandable and immediate the societal structure itself.

There are two such frames with regard to deafness: the framing of the
impairment within a range of normal acceptance, that is, a straightforward
application of the parameters of "normal" socialization; and the framing of
the impairment as a unique sociocultural phenomenon. Frames operate according to rules and may be applied in varieties of transforms. For the purpose of
the present theory, the following rules of applications can be described for the
two frames.

Normal socialization can be applied in either a strong or a weak version.

Acculturation, on the other hand, may assume degrees of passivity or activity. Adaptations to the tensions among the simultaneous presence and availability of the frames may be conceived as resolutions by actors dependent on composite use of the features of the respective frames (see figure 7-1).

Normal Socialization

Several authors have pointed out that the meaning of any departure from a physical state of normality in American society is defined from a medical or pathological standpoint (Manning and Fabrega 1973). Deafness has a structural meaning as a medical problem. However, the diagnosis of deafness does not lead to a straightforward treatment (Meadow 1968). Still, a deaf person may avoid a pathological identity by stressing the medical frame and seeking treatment, which takes the form of "normalization" procedures.[1] These amount to educational and interactive strategies that insist upon the paramount importance of

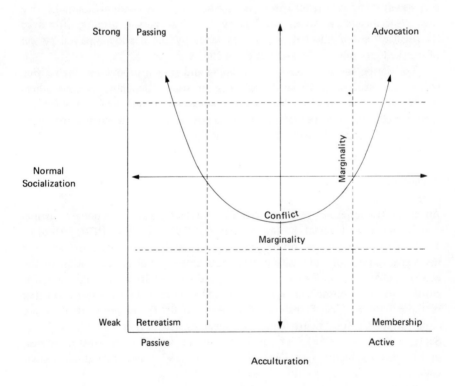

Figure 7-1. Adaptations to Deafness

lipreading and speech production (Uden 1968). "Normality" is defined as an approximation of the actual parameters of normal conversation. Of course, not all hearing-impaired persons learn to speak equally well. Not all have unlimited access to speech therapists who might help them develop what skills they have. All, however, internalize the knowledge that the absence of normal speech stigmatizes them.

It is crucial to the subsequent adaptation of the person with a hearing loss sufficient to affect speech that that person internalize the stigma attached to deafness. In order, to pursue the avenue to normal socialization, one must have accepted the societally framed interpretations that lead to the conclusion that speaking is prerequisite to normality. Hence, the person who relies on hearing aids and conscientiously practices techniques for articulation of speech sounds plays the part of the passive deviant. He or she accepts the interpretation of deafness as abnormal (the stigma of deafness) and attempts to normalize his or her identity through efforts to approximate normal speech performance. But stigma—a discrepancy within the frame—cannot be totally avoided by this strategy since certain aspects of normal English discourse (for example, phonology such as stress and intonation) are never mastered by those with profound hearing loss. Nevertheless, whatever proficiency the deaf person attains, efforts to "normalize" are predicated on an acceptance by the hearing-impaired person of the tacit grounds for the attribution of stigma.

For the person who relies on lipreading and speech production for routine social existence, the successful avoidance of stigma depends on how others perceive his or her communicative performances. A judgment of unproblematic speech comprehension permits a person to pass as normal, whereas a judgment of unintelligible speech discredits the individual.

Acculturation

An alternative interpretive frame requires the deaf person to acquire a distinctive linguistic and social knowledge (Jacobs 1974; Higgins 1979a; Meadow 1972). This process entails both a passive and an active dimension. Although the medical meanings of not hearing may ground the initial interpretation of the aberrant character of the impairment, the dominant feature of this frame is cultural. A consciousness of kind is instilled among those who learn to think of themselves as "deaf." Instead of a treatment for the impairment, there are either strategies for "neutralizing" its meaning (see Sykes and Matza 1957; Scott and Lyman 1968),[2] or for advocating on behalf of the distinctiveness of the cultural reality (see Gussow and Tracy 1971, and their discussion of counterstigma theorizing among lepers).

With the exception of a small number of persons born deaf to deaf parents (less than 10 percent of all persons with a hearing impairment) this "deaf socialization" begins in adolescence, is heavily peer oriented, and focuses around the acquisition of American Sign Language (ASL) within a supportive context, for example, a residential school for the deaf. The distinctiveness of a "visual language" allows for a feeling of membership. Although the mechanism through which visual modes of communication provide for conditions of sociability that are different from the conditions of hearing modes is not fully understood, studies reveal that this socialization process takes place primarily within the visual mode (Cicourel and Boese 1972; Cicourel 1974b).

Although hereditary deafness accounts for only a small proportion of the deaf population, deaf persons born into deaf families represent the purest examples of members of deaf culture. For them and, later in life, for some others with hearing impairments, their language embodies the meanings of everyday life. Within this domain and the horizons of experience it defines, the possibility of "routine" interaction arises (Cicourel 1974a). Routine interaction is grounded in unproblematic enactments of assumptions; in short, enactments are based on appraisals of the other person's intentions such that an action can be performed on the first presumption that it is not, nor will it be regarded as, stigmatizable. Within the culture frame, the stigma of deafness seemingly applies to the entire community and to individuals as representatives of that community. The stigma operates only to the extent that is acknowledged as pertinent to the community by the members. Thus the frame can be said to "neutralize" the spoiling effects of stigma.

Membership (Weak Normalizing and an Active Culture)

Often acculturation also means internalization of a stigma. Although the signs embody the horizons of the deaf experience and the culture acts as buffer to the "spoiling effects" of stigma, the deaf person may not regard ASL as a language of the same stature as English. Stokoe (1970) discusses this situation as a unique manifestation of diglossia. The deaf may encourage their hearing children to use English and, if they have deaf children, may defer to hearing teachers who employ a system of signing that may be influenced more by English than by ASL. A deaf mother of two deaf children comments:

> I can't understand some of the other deaf children. They use SEE [Signing Essential English, a form of signed English], I think. It's okay. My kids are the same, but at home they use regular signs.

A middle-aged man speaking to a group of deaf people at a club meeting:

> It's important for us to learn all of the signs the kids are using at school and sign that way so that they will learn good English. It's

hard, I know, but we will try to organize some classes and learn to use the endings and the invented signs that they use at school. The kids need our help. [Field notes, 1977]

This attitude toward their own diverse linguistic environment reflects weak, normal socialization and subsequent acceptance of stigmatization, coupled with a strong sense of solidarity. In return for the acceptance of the stigma, the deaf person may engage in the action of the community and derive a sense of selfhood essentially from that involvement. It is in contacts with the hearing that the neutralizing effects of this strategy can be observed.

Sidney (35 years of age) works in a print shop with several other deaf people. His supervisor is hearing and does not know sign language. Sidney's parents sent him to a residential school for the deaf at an early age. He does not trust his lipreading ability for important matters, and he prefers not to use his voice. He is sure it sounds strange to hearing people. So, he usually writes notes to Mr. Sparks, the supervisor, who nods or writes a message back. On weekends Sidney and his wife may drive several hundred miles to visit deaf friends. Sometimes he is frustrated by his inability to communicate with hearing people. But mostly he can avoid them. Note writing works, but sometimes he can't spell and he thinks maybe they don't understand his awkward English. Really he feels pretty lucky to have a job and good deaf friends around the country. [Field notes, 1978]

The following characteristics mark the membership adaptation:

1. ASL embodies the horizons of the experience (Cicourel and Boese 1972).
2. The influence of deaf peers becomes disproportionate to societally derived influences (Padden and Markowicz 1976; Meadow 1977).
3. There is a heightened level of social participation among "kind" that appears to be more pronounced than general patterns of social participation among the "normal" population (Schein and Delk 1974).
4. Involvement in the community seems to neutralize the effects of the stigma on the person while he or she is engaged in participation within the boundaries of the community. The existence of the community and membership in it do not call into question the general meanings of the stigma.

Advocating (Strong Normalizing and an Active Culture)

An active acculturation experience can combine with strong, normal socialization to generate ingenious adaptations, which often take the form of advocating or counterstigma theorizing (Gussow and Tracy 1971). Within or parallel to the culture there develop groups of people who espouse a "counterstigma theory" that denies the dominant frame for deafness and advocates new means for achieving full and equal participation in society. The young, the educated, the elite are the vanguard of this innovative adaptation (Stokoe, Bernard, and Padden 1976). Advocating is an innovative response to the dominant or normal framing of the meanings of deafness. Not only do these innovators use ASL but they also regard the imposition of spoken English in their lives as discriminatory. Deafness, they assert, should not be regarded as an incurable consequence of aberrations of hearing but, rather, as a viable alternative social existence.

Medical-pathological meanings are refuted and openly rejected by these persons. Their response, however, is not rebellious (see Merton 1963) since they compare their life-style to that of other minorities (Erting 1978) and simply extend a "frame of equality" to cover accidents of birth and fate other than skin color, mother tongue, and sexual preferences.

Following the lead of other civil-rights movements, they demonstrate and may actually seek conflict with the hearing in order to assert the worth of the deaf culture, the beauty and nativity of their often newly discovered language, and the legitimacy of their means of participating in society. Advocates make presentations before civic groups and serve on committees and commissions. Their causes range from establishing training and credentialing for adequate signing in the schools, interpreting services, educational opportunities, and employment-related services, to captoning for television and representation in legislative bodies. Symbolized by bumper stickers and pins reading "deaf power" or "deaf pride," this movement encourages deaf people to aspire to the general goals of independence and self-reliance that frame the meanings of everyday life in American society. Those who adopt this adaptation aim for entrance to business, professional, and academic circles *as deaf individuals.*

Experience in the deaf culture leads these persons to evaluate their membership in positive terms. They do not neutralize their potential stigma through avoidance or accommodation; instead, they confront derogatory interpretations and construct a rationale for refuting them, an alternative framing device. If the stigma that derives from medical interpretations can be reevaluated as representing political, linguistic, and cultural problems, and if redress can be made for these putative inequalities, then the stigma can be successfully removed.

A young deaf advocate outlines his views:

It is very difficult to get the deaf to speak up for themselves, to stand up for their rights. How can we raise their awareness? They can't hear. But with interpreters the deaf can handle situations where they need to speak for themselves. With interpreters they can enter the mainstream of society at all levels. We need the support of hearing people, need to find out what works best to sensitize them. Of course, if it requires tact, results may be slow. Less tact may result in more honest relationships, more effective and more immediate changes. We need organization. The individual activist becomes a one-man show and may be criticized by many within the deaf community. An organization of the deaf at the local and state levels is the best vehicle for change. But many of the already existing organizations are ineffective because of conservative leadership, conflicts and tensions between old and young, working class and those with higher education and language skills. The key is involvement of the deaf as a group in change in schools, jobs, and professional research. Many hearing professionals are afraid to support getting the deaf into the professions because they would be out of a job! [Interview, 1978]

Activists may represent only a small portion of the deaf community. Since their mentality is one of assertiveness from the vantage point of many, advocating can pose a threat to solidarity since, as shown previously, such solidarity depends to some extent on the internalization of stigmatization. Hence, the advocator may encounter difficulty in mobilizing support for even the most-basic causes of equality, such as equal opportunity or access to educational institutions, from well-entrenched community members. To the "member" such innovation can only operate to undermine the grounds for reciprocity among the deaf. Such members are uncomfortable in the hearing world and do not wish to join it, even with "equal opportunities." (A manifestation of this conflict has been documented by Padden and Markowicz [1976], in their identification of relationships among students at a college for the deaf. These conflicts take place largely between members or advocates, on the one side, and passers and retreatists on the other.)

A characterization of the adaptation of advocators would include the following.

1. The use of the language of the deaf as a culturally pure form (Klima and Bellugi 1979), with ASL is defended as both art and culture and extolled for its function in establishing membership and identity.
2. Acceptance of goals of independence, equality, and participation in mainstream society.
3. The tension between normal socialization and acculturation manifests itself in conflict both within the deaf culture and between the deaf and the hearing.
4. The vanguard of innovative responses assumes the form of counterstigma theorizing or advocative strategies.

Passing (Strong Normalizing and Passive Culture)

The deaf person can never completely hide behind the skills of lipreading and speech production. There are too many conditions of social interaction in which overheard, out-of-sight conversations and subtle nonverbal clues play an important role (see Goodwin 1979). However, one adaptation to the potential stigmatization of not hearing is to assume an attitude in which one tries to behave as if he or she can hear. The person thinks ahead about the nature of interaction, guesses what a hearing person would do or say, and then acts on the basis of these guesses. This pattern is exemplified in the hearing family's encounter with Nicky:

> One night when our family was having dinner out, we noticed a young woman watching us from across the room. We are used to that because our ten-year-old daughter is deaf, and we all sign to each other so she will not miss out on the conversation. We are an unusual sight. But this woman was wearing a hearing aid, so we had decided she was probably deaf, too.
>
> After a few minutes she came to our table and introduced herself as Nicky Adams. She explained that she is deaf, but never learned sign language.
>
> "My mother and father worked with me and sent me to the best private schools. I had speech and lipreading training. It was very hard, but it was worth it. Now I am a college student. And I get along very well."
>
> We complimented her on her speech and lipreading skill. She was remarkable. I didn't really believe she couldn't hear our voices. Then my three-year-old, who had been quietly waiting for his food decided to join her conversation. "Hi," he said, "I'm Mike and I ordered french fries." Since he had chosen to share with Nicky this bit of news that was completely out of context, she looked at me puzzled and a bit embarrassed. I quickly explained what Mike had said. She was very good, but now we were sure she was really deaf. The momentary loss of context for the conversation had confused her. [Field notes, 1978]

As the studies of the tacit grounds of conversational exchange indicate, meaning is realized through a negotiation between partners regarding intentions and use of presumed background knowledge (Cicourel 1974a; Psathas 1979). The "passing" adult is at an obvious disadvantage in this exchange. Without full access to all the channels of conversational meaning, he or she always faces the possibility of an exposure of the stigmatizable trait.

As Goffman (1963) has pointed out, one strategy is to avoid situations of exposure. To a person who cannot hear, this means restricting the circle of interactants to those who know that he or she cannot hear and who will not use the stigma associated with the condition against him or her. Nicky, for example, was protected by the knowledge that the family had a deaf child and would "understand." Ironically, it is through the tacit acknowledgment of the stigma that the stigma can be ignored and the person's condition normalized. The oral adult relies on hearing people who are "wise" (Goffman 1963, pp. 19-31) to their condition to serve as companions in the management of the

environment of passing. Again, such a view of the nature of everyday life rests
on a passive acceptance of the societal definition of not hearing. The aberration
of not hearing becomes understandable as a deviation from normality; and the
person who attempts to talk, even if without lucidity, does not constitute a
threat to conceptions of normality. He or she has acknowledged that normal
speech is prerequisite to full personhood and that since that "normality" cannot
be achieved totally, the approximation of it affords the greatest opportunities
for participation in society, albeit participation as a stigmatized individual.

Merton (1963, p. 149) observes that ritualistic types of adaptation involve
the abandoning or scaling down of "lofty cultural goals." Since normality is,
by definition, an unattainable goal, the strategy of passing may be seen as a
ritualistic practice. It requires the enactment of taken-for-granted knowledge
even though the purposes of those framing assumptions are displaced or forgotten (Goffman 1974). The problematic character of everyday interaction
is normally habituated through an objectification whereby the assumptions
about what constitutes routine action become "real in their consequences"
(Berger and Luckmann 1967). Frames form in order to render unnecessary a
perpetual starting from scratch. However, the insistence that the deaf act on
these "hearing frames" is tantamount to a "scaling down of lofty cultural
goals." A deaf person's act of passing is a symbolic affirmation of institutionalized means of interaction devoid of any goal of full participation.

In summary, characteristics of passing include:

1. Ritualism.
2. Heightened conflict owing to denials of the deaf culture and to the ever-
    present risk of being found out.
3. A dependence on hearing people both in the management of information
    about potential discreditability and in the implementation of normal
    frames.
4. Dominance of English and subsequent refutation or ignoring of ASL.

Retreating (Weak Normalizing and Passive Culture)

Merton's classic description of retreating stresses a motivational shutdown
on the part of the individual. "People who adapt (or maladapt) in this fashion
are, strictly speaking *in* the society but not *of* it" (Merton 1963, p. 153). He
lists defectism, quietism, and resignation as individual retreatist responses to
the "dilemma either of being crushed in the struggle to achieve" or "of
succumbing to a hopeless resignation and flight from" the act of trying to
succeed (Gardiner 1945, quoted in Merton 1963, p. 155). Retreatists are
socially disinherited; and, with regard to the deaf, the collective adaptation
they made is the epitome of the "dependent, handicapped person."

The hearing-impaired person faces a dilemma between either becoming a fully deaf person—a member of the deaf community—or struggling toward an approximation of normality. Advocating represents a positive or active negotiation of this tension by merging the institutionalized deaf modes and cultural goals of normality under a larger interpretation of equality. Retreatism embodies a negative resolution. The retreatist gives up and clings to the minimal support system that has been established through family ties and, more recently, the welfare state. The retreatist may have learned some signs, but the communicative system he uses reflects the dominance of English. Many may have attempted other adaptations but, for various reasons, have withdrawn from contacts with the deaf or the "wise" among the hearing. Typically, persons whose response is retreatist were born of hearing parents. The patterned social actions they pursue and the interdependency they have accomplished through intercessors constitute the means by which they may retreat from full social participation.

> Linda is 43 years old. She lives with her mother who is 68. Never married, she held a job as a teacher of the deaf at a state school briefly. She resigned and returned to live with her widowed mother. Since she turned 28 she has lived "at home," and she and her mother have survived from the inheritance left by her father, who was a lawyer. Linda is a fine artist, but she has never shown an interest in a public display of her works. She is well-educated, well-read, and very polite. She confides to having "no real friends." She learned "signed English" while a teacher and uses it with simultaneous speech when conversing with hearing people who she knows can sign and when contacting other deaf people, usually through government agencies. Otherwise, her routine life affairs are conducted through her difficult, strained speech. Her life is very routine and isolated. [Field notes, 1978]

Certainly, retreatist adaptations can assume many forms. All, however, essentially entail:

1. A weak resolve to use the "frame of normality" in efforts to pass as hearing.
2. Passive application of the values of the "frame of deafness," either as an accomplished membership to neutralize the stigma or as a distinctive cultural ideology.
3. Minimization of conflict while influences from the hearing world dominate.
4. Accentuation of social isolation.

Conflict and Marginality

Conflict among the frames of interpretations may be represented by opposing renditions of the meanings given by society and tensions between active and passive adaptations. As with any set of structural discontinuities, marginal adaptations are possible. Marginality may be regarded as descriptive of the relationships between normal and acculturalized socialization. As Sussman (1965) suggests, marginal adaptations represent the situation of many deaf people as they feel themselves caught between two opposing modes for establishing the meanings of not hearing. Of course, retreatist resolutions may be made; but many do not opt for such adaptations. Instead, they may seek to use the two framing devices in varying degrees, thereby situating themselves between the two positions.

As Coser (1956) would no doubt remark, the conflict generated from a stance of advocacy does have functional consequences for the whole culture as solidarity increases among those who fight for equality. However, these increases in solidarity can polarize the community itself, as active and passive types find themselves at odds. Further, as Goffman (1963) has demonstrated, passing heightens conflict between one's discreditable condition and one's appearance.

However, more-subtle relationships are embodied within the experience of marginality. That experience occurs in the interstices of passive-active and strong-weak responses. The experience of marginality stems from two conditions: (1) the person's socialization does not place him or her completely either in a state of normality or in full membership in the deaf culture, and (2) the two states are in some sense antagonistic (Stonequist 1937). Passing means "success" in appearance, whereas membership requires "successful" negotiation of social relationships; advocating necessitates a management of tension between the two states, whereas retreating entails a withdrawal from the dilemma.

Marginal social existence seems to be structurally inherent in the adaptations. Passing is never completely attainable; membership is always achieved within the horizons of the more-general, hearing society; advocating raises the specter of rejection by both the hearing and the deaf. Retreatism, finally, is in itself a kind of marginal mode (Merton 1963). Whenever individuals anticipate in their own behavior the values and actions of members of a reference group to which they aspire and to which they are, by virtue of circumstances beyond their control, ineligible for membership, the consequence is often marginality (Merton 1963, pp. 266, 290).

Further, to have been deprived of normal socialization into a culture—as is the case with all but those born deaf to deaf parents—and to have assimilated the basic values of the dominant hearing culture makes it less than likely that an individual will achieve a full native sense of deaf membership. The concept of marginality, therefore, that turns out to be the most-powerful theoretical device for understanding the deaf experience within an action frame of reference.

A Case of Marginality

Marge was born of very bright, perceptive, hearing parents. She was the first child, and her parents were attuned to her every response or lack of response. Her failure to respond to the telephone ringing or to loud discussions near her crib led to an examination by an ear specialist when she was five or six months old. The diagnosis was congenital "nerve deafness." Then came the round of doctors, the varying diagnoses, and finally the admission that the child could not hear and probably never would. Deafness. What does it mean? The parents dwelled for months and even years on the question of what caused the deafness. There was, of course, no definitive answer. After much emotional turmoil and personal stress, the parents at last focused on the central concern: "How can Marge live as normal a life as possible?"

The search for help led to the Volta Review and to the Volta Bureau, with its helpful tips on lipreading and the importance of early and intense training in oral skills. After her family moved to a city where a "fine, oral school" existed, Marge began her "special education." Her parents enrolled her at the age of three. After she had "adjusted" to school life, her first few words began to emerge—*mama, doggie, bye-bye*. Her parents rewarded these speech attempts and, following the advice of the Tracy correspondence course, maintained a strict discipline over her. They carefully intervened on her behalf, often standing behind her and telling others what she was saying. They carried on this practice so that "she would not be dependent on us as interpreters and because we want her to have confidence in her speaking ability."

Marge was carefully guided to believe that she spoke well, even though her parents admitted that her speaking was often unintelligible and could be understood only by heavy reliance on knowledge of the context of the message. However, Marge was regarded as a model student; and her speech production skills were extolled through an article in a magazine with national circulation. Her early training was typical: a controlled hearing environment with firm but supportive parents. Marge's early training had the effect of isolating her from the deaf community and creating a self-awareness based on her ability to speak and to be understood through the use of speech that sounded like everyone else's. Thus Marge thought of herself as a "normal person." That impression was maintained through judicious management of her environment so that her difference from others was either hidden altogether or minimized. Her teachers acted as agents of control, rewarding her actions only when they approximated their conception of the world of normal existence. Thus, whenever the child emitted speech-like sounds, she was rewarded with candy and with praise: "That is good language" or "Good try!" or "That's good speech." Marge did not think of herself as *essentially* different from normal people. The more successful her training—and Marge's was very successful—the more genuine her conviction that she was not really different from others, just in need of some special training. She was on the path to a normal life.

Marge's amenability to such training was a function of her parents' concern and of teaching efforts, which together produced an environment that managed to sustain a fundamentally unreal self-conception (Meadow 1969). Often people so trained live with parents until long past the time when "normal" children would leave home, marry, start their own families, or start their own lives independent of their parents in terms of identity and economic support. However, as an adolescent Marge decided to try to "make it on her own." She left home, moved to the big city, and started looking for a job. Gradually, she began to see that she was not "normal." This does not mean that she had previously been unaware that she could not hear. But it means that she was not aware of the differences between the deaf and the hearing; she thought that no significant differences existed between these two worlds. She had difficulty both in understanding what was being said to her and in making herself understood. Away from the supportive environment of her parents and the school, her image of herself as a hearing person began to crumble. Frustration after frustration in employment, in friendships, and in courtship with hearing males began to mount. Finally, with her "hearing self-image" in disarray, through a chance meeting she was invited to attend a deaf club's regular gathering. There she met a deaf man who was an important leader in the deaf community. Her speech skills were interpreted by the deaf man as positive attributes, and they could communicate sufficiently to make a date. Marge attended the club meeting and discovered that her speaking skills were of little value there. She was treated cordially, but she sensed that she was an outsider. What she did not know was that for the young deaf man, a deaf woman with "good" speech and talking abilities represented quite a catch.

After a short courtship, Marge and her new-found friend were married. For Marge the marriage meant an introduction to the world of the deaf. Her new husband was a high-status member of this world, and Marge was impressed. A new dimension of life was opened up to her. The marriage was a link, a doorway to an identity as a person, the creation of a new image more realistically grounded in a social group. To the husband, Marge was seen as a link to the hearing world. She was seen as a person who had been successful, who had already proved herself in an alien world, and who would round out the needs of a deaf person forced to live among the hearing. Thus began Marge's introduction to the deaf world. At first there was a period of awakening—learning that conversation could be complete and effortless; sensing what was involved in full social participation; learning the details of social interaction, joking, friendship, community. Marge was a newcomer, and her new husband was the teacher opening the way to new experiences. By her own admission, she began for the first time to understand, to experience human emotion in concert with other humans. She eagerly looked forward to learning new signs; meeting new deaf people; joining the club; going on picnics, outings, and other recreational activities of the deaf. But soon the haunting images of the hearing person within her appeared over the scene. Marge was not a deaf person inside. Inside, she still believed that speaking was a "better" way to communicate than signing. She did not see the signs as "language" equal to English. She tended to be sloppy with her signing, never becoming a "native signer."

When she gave birth to hearing children, she insisted on language tutoring for them and on generally conducting the family's affairs in spoken English. She tried to create a hearing home environment, thinking that only in this way could her children learn English and, hence, become normal persons. Further, she believed that her English skills were sufficient to accomplish these objectives. Therefore, she attempted to teach her children English, using the same approaches that her mother had used with her. The result was a linguistic barrier between parents and children. The father became the deaf person and the mother the hearing. This situation was greatly complicated by Marge's insistence that English be spoken to the children. For Marge, the signs were a language of pathology. She had assigned her husband to a subordinate role in the raising of their children, and her actions and attitudes became a wedge between the father and his children. Growing estrangement between parents and children led ultimately to psychiatric intervention, divorce, and a court fight over the custody of the children.

Marginality as a Way of Life

The dysfunctional consequences of marginality are well documented (Stonequist 1937; Merton 1963, pp. 265, 266). Still, as can be seen in connection with intellectuals (Seeman 1956) and with extension to other adaptations made by certain minority groups, marginal status can stimulate creative and adjustive adaptations to discrimination. Merton (1963, p. 266) writes that in an open social system a marginal status can allow anticipatory socialization to take place, enhancing participation in a higher-status grouping. Such socialization amounts to a defection from the original stance. However, whenever participation is less than total in either level and opportunities for entrance at the lower level remain open, marginality may represent an acculturation avenue leading (for the deaf) both to a degree of membership in the deaf community and to a degree of participation in the hearing world.

The case of Marge illustrates this possibility. After a very difficult period following her divorce, she met, courted and married a well-educated deaf man whose English proficiency and whose high status in both the deaf community and the broader educational organizations administering to the deaf lessened the conflict between Marge's previous socialization and her interpretation of the deaf community. His "elite" status could accommodate her views of the hearing and the deaf worlds, and he could use his high status as a device for introducing her to an alternative evaluation of deafness. Marge regained custody of her children and has remained married for several years; she is active in social life among the "educated" deaf in her community. She still cultivates relationships with hearing people, but these efforts are stylistically more appropriate in her new context.

Implications and Conclusions

Without a general theoretical scheme, the significance of isolated research findings can be missed. Subsuming research questions under models that stress psychological or linguistic explanatory conceptions can also mask insights of a sociological nature. The suggestion of an action theory of deafness can explicate consequences of adaptations that have been either overlooked or obscured by preoccupation with other concerns. By relating the insights of an action perspective to four areas of current research, the usefulness of the proposed general theorizing can be demonstrated.

First, concern for the mental-health problems of the deaf, particularly of deaf children, has burgeoned (Schlesinger and Meadow 1972; Trybus 1977; Montgomery 1978). Typically, the causes of these problems are traced to consequences of language and social deprivation. Often, however, less-than-straightforward associations are reported; and antedotal accounts may attribute causality to hearing parents, implying that in order to "save" the children, the parents must be educated to appreciate the "reality" of deafness. An action perspective reveals that aligning actions are endemic to the experience of deafness and, ironically, that advocacy might heighten the dilemma in a manner similar to that suggested by the societal-reaction theory regarding passing adaptations. Rather than assuming that it has been a normalizing interpretive process that has isolated the deaf (especially children of hearing parents), it may now be necessary to look for interactive alignments and to be aware of the more-subtle phenomena of marginality. Further, assumptions regarding the dysfunctional consequences of marginality may not be warranted. Research, then, could be directed at assessing the mental-health implications of the peculiar existence of deaf people. This theoretical expression of the forces involved in negotiating the meanings of the impairment states that marginality may represent an optimal adaptation, that is, one that avoids the risks of the extreme strategies of either of the interpretive frames.

Second, questions of the nature and extent of deviance among the deaf can be addressed within this framework. Conventional wisdom and first-hand contact with the deaf leads to the impression that they are conservative (almost reactionary) in attitudes toward race, sexuality, drug use, and questions of social change. However, Zakarewsky (1979) has documented the existence of deaf-gay groups whose attempts to join with national movements have been met with less than enthusiasm by hearing gay people. The deaf, gay person, therefore, seems to manifest the general dynamics of adaptations sketched here, plus an ideology of a "deviant" movement. Hence, such persons' gay liaisons are endogomous and involve a double stigma (gay and deaf). In addition they are stigmatized by "straight," deaf people (Woodward's 1979 presentation of the signs of sexual behavior show that signs used by the deaf to denote homosexual behavior are often iconic and quite derogatory). Studying deviance among the deaf could inform as well as be informed by traditional sociological concepts.

Third, the limits of an ethnolinguistic model for the understanding of deafness can be identified through this perspective. The convincing evidence about the natural character of signs does not warrant conclusions about its use. A full analysis of the extension of notions of equality must account for the various meanings for and adaptations to deafness. Likewise, tracing the patterns of diglossia, pidgins, and other sociolinguistic phenomena does not fully explicate the multifaceted problems of the introduction of bilingualism as a policy (Erting 1978; see Grimshaw 1979). Conceiving of deafness ethnolinguistically does represent a major and impressive accomplishment. However, the range of social phenomena accompanying deafness can not be subsumed under this rubric alone. The examination of adaptations, although not refuting the ethnolinguistic perspective, does go beyond it to posit a basic sociological question: How may interactions be accomplished when social structure provides the actor with dilemmas of choices, and what are the consequences of various negotiations of the structure?

Finally, the deaf community has been described as socioeconomically working class (Becker 1978; Moore 1978). Levels of education, types of occupations, and underrepresentation in the professions all reflect profiles that are symptomatic of oppressed opportunity (Rainwater 1974). As Merton himself pointed out, dispositions toward adaptive action are conditioned by class. The grid (figure 7-1) portrays a theoretical description. Application in everyday-life situations as well as the formulation of several policies, for instance, would certainly manifest the effects of larger sociological forces. Merton suggested that ritualistic adaptations would be prevalent among the lower middle classes, whereas innovative responses would be typically lower middle class. Of course, an adaptation to deafness confounds a direct association with class. Nevertheless, preliminary observations and available data warrant the conclusion that *membership* is an adaptation of truncated opportunities, whereas *passing* seems to characterize middle- and upper-class responses. Private oral schools and celebrities who take up the cause of deafness stress passing adapatations, whereas *retreatism* as a protective strategy is predicated on economic and social wherewithal. Finally, *advocating,* the most-recent form, seems to be an upper-middle-class response.

Current data are merely suggestive of class configurations associated with adaptations, and future research will be required to depict the precise patterns. Conceptualizing adaptations as action patterns promises to open new and rich vistas of inquiry. The scope of an action perspective allows an assessment of the impairment to be brought back in (Higgins 1980b) without reducing the study of deafness to linguistics, applications of psychological theories, or descriptions of problem solving in everyday life. Further, sociological theory, as Sussman advised, can inform other disciplinary perspectives to provide a comprehensive understanding of the social phenomena of deafness.

Notes

1. The use of *normalization* in this sense means that the parents and family of the deaf child, for example, attempt to train the child in the skills necessary for appearing as if he or she were hearing. Although the deaf person rarely succeeds in passing, trying to pass means that he or she is acknowledging what is "normal" and is fulfilling an obligation to approximate normality. The socialization of the deaf child is carried out in a home environment and a school situation in which parents and teachers refuse to class the child with "the deaf." For a similar usage, see Haber and Smith (1971).

2. Our use of *neutralization*, although specific to the group we are studying, owes some of its meaning to Matza's original formulation (Matza 1964; Sykes and Matza 1957). The neutralizing deaf person acknowledges the abnormality of deafness; but instead of trying to "right" himself by learning to be hearing, he denies the applicability of speech and oral skills to himself and withdraws into a supportive subculture where his manual language is adequate for a full life. He is deaf; therefore, he has no responsibility to be hearing. This adaptation loosens the control of the hearing world over him.

8 Societal Change and the Deaf Community

Several recent and excellent descriptions of the community of the deaf are now available (Higgins 1980a; Jacobs 1974). Higgins's work stands out as being particularly attuned to sociological conceptions of community. This chapter supplements his efforts and addresses questions of social change that implicate the deaf community.

Directionality in the Trends toward Modern Society

In one of his most-audacious undertakings, Parsons (1966, 1971) attempted to take up the task set by Max Weber, namely, to chronicle, describe, and explain the emergence of modern society. Parsons clearly thought of "western society in the modern era as of 'universal' significance in human history and in the corollary of that judgment: that the development of modern society has not been random but definitely directional" (1971, p. 139).

Surely one of the most-troublesome conceptions of twentieth-century social theory has been that of modernity, with its derivative questions about the nature of community. Nisbet regards the history of Western social philosophy to be concerned basically with "ideas and ideals of community." He uses the word *community* to refer to a "lasting sense of relationship among individuals that are characterized by a high degree of personal intimacy, of social cohesion or moral commitment, and of continuity in time" (Nisbet 1973, p. 1). As Nisbet notes, the grounds on which this sense of community can be built may vary along a remarkably complex array, from sexual preference to royal lineage. Nevertheless, amid this complexity some scholars have painstakingly isolated features that putatively establish the grounds for a division of communities along a directional continuum toward increasingly modern criteria.

What Is Modern Community?

Now-classic social-science literature, like the writings of Toennies, documents a dramatic shift over the last century in the quality of and the foundations for Western community. Toennies conceived of this shift not so much as a continuous movement from emotive, stable, territorial criteria toward rational,

malleable, and amphorous bases, but rather as a concomitant increase in the
"kinds" of associations (*gesellschaft*) in which people could engage, and the
dialectic between this tendency and the anchored permanence of the traditional
community (*gemeinschaft*). Modern society clearly stresses the individual's
ability to interact according to a "calculus" of exchange. This emphasis has
come at the expense of spontaneous feelings, contiguity, and the stability of
the territorially defined sense of homeland.

Traditional communities, as Weber and Redfield show, each in his own
way, can be quite strong and can continue as long as their environments supply
a sufficiently supportive flow of resources. Indeed, some studies of folk society
seem to idealize its balance between nature and society. Still, most of the
earlier sociologists such as Weber, Durkheim, and Simmel were astonished at the
vulnerability of the traditional community to modern social forces. To Weber,
this vulnerability yielded kin and territory to rationalization and its organizational scion, the bureaucracy. Modern life became newly routinized, demysti-
fied, temporal, and open to forces such as alienation, isolation, normlessness,
and unscrupulous charismatic types.

Early social thinkers made a mixed judgment of the new, industrialized,
Western society. According to Simmel, the level of excitement found only in
the new urban life-styles could prove quite stimulating to the intellect. Even
Weber's remorse gave way on occasion to a depiction of new social orders
bright with increased individual freedom.

It was Parsons who, over several decades (1951, 1966), described the
dilemmas and tensions of modern life most graphically. He did so through
the use of an analytic device abstracted from the classical sociological literature. Part of this device he called the *patterned variables*. Parsons chose to
conceive of the *qualitative* features of social action as continua. These are
five: achievement versus ascription; emotional involvement versus emotional
neutrality; self-defined versus collectively defined interests; specificity versus
diffuseness; and universal versus particular meanings for social action (see
Turner 1978, pp. 48-51).

Throughout his descriptions of family interaction, bureaucratic life, and
educational settings—and more globally in his identification of *directionality*
in modern social change—Parsons stresses achievement over ascription, emotional neutrality over emotional involvement, self-interest over collective
interest, specifically focused action over the diffuse usage of the person, and
particular meanings for actions in place of universal meanings. To Parsons,
one could talk of a typically modern pattern of social action. However, as
with Toennies, Durkheim, and Weber, these trends did not mean the emergence of a unidimensional modern personality. Rather, the modern personality
and its supportive context, the community, would both reflect and induce
tension among all five simultaneously occurring features. Features characteristic of traditional communities would not disappear from modern society,

but their manifestation would be more circumscribed. Emotional expressivity, for instance, although still essential to social life, would become confined to ever more narrowly defined contexts. Indeed, the description Parsons relates is one of complex dynamics within a constantly changing matrix of qualitative meanings for social life. Out of this dynamic emerges a consistent pattern that reflects a direction toward the rational, instrumental meaning of action.

The impact of the forces of modernization on the individual point up not only an interdependency within society but also a capability in people to make sense of their participation in society. Within increasingly segmental roles, the inhabitant of modern society exists in and is surrounded by small worlds (Luckmann 1978). Berger and his colleagues (Berger, Berger, and Kellner 1973) regard some characteristics of modern consciousness as intrinsic to the "modes of production" in a highly technological economy. However, they treat other characteristics as derived from influences not necessarily essential to the economy or its organization, referring to these as extrinsic. There can be little doubt that people habituated to the small worlds of their private existence and overwhelmed by the complexity of larger social horizons form associations that are specific to interests and relatively temporary. Keyes (1973) captured the dilemma of modern community in his title *We, the Lonely People.* Both the appeal of alternative life-styles and our ambivalence toward the experience of strong communal associations are connected to our awareness that communities of unassimilated persons seem fueled by real or imagined oppression and by the conscious avoidance of mainstream trends.

The Deaf Community

Elsewhere we quoted a depiction of the deaf community as a "natural consequence of uninhibited communication" (Jacobs 1974). Three features of the association of deaf people seem to account for their "lasting sense of relationship" (Nisbet 1973). First, like many communities that have resisted or have only belatedly begun to come under the influence of modern social forces, there is a linguistic dimension to belonging. Sharing a language, as we have repeatedly noted, can engender a strong feeling of relationship. Second, as Higgins (1980a, b) has documented, is the specialized knowledge deaf people have as the result of having experienced both stigmatization and impaired capabilities to cope with the problems of everyday life. The result of these inextricably linked conditions is a shared knowledge about the meaning of suffering, a sense that only those who are deaf can deeply understand the difficulties of "making it" in a hearing world. Third, simply being outside the hearing society shapes a view of the world, which we have described as *consciousness.*

In this sociological sense, the deaf community is certainly a viable entity, standing as a minority group among other minority groups. However, it has features that are, if not unique, at least quite distinctive, which define its relationship to larger societal structures. Members of the deaf community typically enter the community late in life. Most deaf persons, of course, have hearing parents. Perforce, they are not ascribed a membership in the community of the deaf but must achieve that acceptance chiefly through demonstration of sign-language skills and the expression of proper attitudes and knowledge about everyday problems. That is, they must know what it means to be deaf according to an adult version of common-sense knowledge and must express themselves within an approved idiom.

Many members of various kinds of communities—gays, ecologists, and so forth—also achieve membership late in life and also must demonstrate proper attitudes and the correct medium of discourse. However, the traditional community does not function in this manner. Rather, it contains among its ranks a full age range, with rites of passage marking movement within the structure of the community. The deaf community, by contrast, seems to be highly segregated by age. Children are either at home with their hearing parents or together only at school; young adults are "on their own" with their own kind. Finally, old people live among themselves in special facilities. Thus the deaf community rarely bands together for events that join all ages. Obviously, this tendency is due to the influences of education and to the mixing of hearing and deaf persons in the kinship setting. In this regard, the deaf community appears to fall well within the scope of "modern" community.

Rarely researched but clearly pertinent is the question of what effect late entry into a "sign community" has on the composition of that community. Deaf people typically learn signs after, or at least relatively far into, what psycholinguists call the *critical period* (McNeill 1966; DeVillers and DeVillers 1979). By this they mean the period of early life (two to eight years of age) in which the majority of language learning takes place. Meadow (1980) summarizes much of the research on language acquisition among deaf children. With the exception of deaf children born deaf to deaf parents—and even then only if the parents sign freely, spontaneously, and naturally to their children—most children born deaf or deafened in childhood do not "see" much "natural" signing.

The circumstances under which sign is learned are at the residential school, during adolescent recreation, and the leisure-time activities of early adulthood. Although the literature on the nature of first-language acquisition when a person has been deprived of a natural language until an older age is far from definitive, the case of Genie seems to indicate that certain language incompetencies and performances may characterize late first-language acquisition (Curtiss 1977). This literature would suggest, at least, that variety and variation of sign skills and styles of performance would be quite large among those who enter a linguistic community late. This state of affairs contrasts markedly with that of most ethnic and racial communities, where the language of the community is acquired at a normal stage of life. In having late-learning "natives" making up the major proportion of its membership, the deaf community is unique.

Higgins (1980a) downplays the importance of sign-language skills and emphasizes the social sense of identity in his description of the deaf community. Perhaps, if such tolerance of variety does exist, it is due to the actual "abnormal" range of skills found among the deaf and to the efforts by the deaf to manage various circles of signers within the larger community context. The existence of such a situation would mean that knowledge of "sameness" sufficient to produce a strong sense of identity overrides the presumption of a wide-based competency in a natural language that usually characterizes an ethnic community. The deaf simply cannot afford the selectivity of membership that a rigid criterion of linguistic competency would produce.

Third, the deaf community has little or no territorial identity. Territory, however, need not be thought of as a static location. As Lyman and Scott (1970) convincingly argue, *territory* can be a useful concept when it is coupled with *interaction*. Thus an analyst can conceive of the "space" within which an interaction takes place. Interactants themselves establish a territory and carry it about, creating it anew with each encounter. Still, the traditional community profits greatly from a fixed location or "turf." Certainly, such a space changes with ecological processes of invasion and succession; but this space functions as a platform, a stage on which activities that encompass a full range of life transpire. Gans's (1962) work, *The Urban Villagers*, stresses the stability that inhabitants of the "Italian part" of town feel from having become accustomed to a particular setting or landscape. So salient is the dimension of setting, according to the Bergers, that "when sociologists speak about the community, one may usually substitute the term human landscape to make what they are saying more graphic" (Berger and Berger 1972, p. 101).

The deaf community has no landscape. Hence, its territory is inextricably linked to interaction; it is a symbolic community, a network of associations that places a premium on values. These include values toward ASL as a "noble" language and negative values toward the "talk" of "hearies" and educators, as well as strong social ties, the result of conscious efforts to come together in bonds of friendship woven from the signs (see Padden 1980).

Fourth, unlike the traditional community, the deaf community has few or poorly developed institutional supports. Family, economic, religious, and political institutional forms make up a closely interconnected web in ethnic and racial communities. Urban society weakens these interrelationships and their mutually supporting effects on institutional life. In the case of the deaf, those links that exist at all are fragmented and often conflictual. Principally, the institutions implicated in the deaf community are the family, religion, education, and government.

The family of the deaf person typically comprises hearing persons. The deaf themselves tend to marry late in life. They must leave their families to become involved in the community. They frequent clubs and join activity-oriented groups such as bowling leagues, ski clubs, and snowmobile associations. These involvements entail primarily leisure-time activities. Until they do marry, deaf persons typically operate out of a hearing home peopled by others who rarely do more than acquiesce to the possibility of a "deaf way of life."

Educational institutions have almost always been controlled by hearing people. Top-level administrative positions are held by the hearing, the majority of teachers are hearing and the dominance of English is strong and easily discernible to the deaf person.

Historically, conservative or fundamentalist religious institutions have provided a safe haven for sociability among the deaf. But religion is to a large extent inherited, that is, passed on from parent to child. Most deaf children have hearing parents, and with few exceptions church membership in the United States has not kept pace with population growth. Fewer and fewer persons attend church or report any church affiliation. Especially among young adults, church attendance has dropped radically over a twenty-year period. Church goers seem to be the very young and the very old (see Alston 1975). The practical consequences of this tendency toward the secularization of religious beliefs are the subject of a sociology of religion. Certainly, no sociologist would argue that religion is no longer a potent social force in modern society; but the belief systems that make up the "sacred canopy" of society have been transformed into a variety of movements and modes of expression (Berger 1968; Yinger 1957; Lofland 1978). The plain fact emerges that the organized church is simply not in a position to administer broadly to the deaf community, at least not to a community that would include a wide range of age and of other demographic features.

Finally, government support for deaf people in the areas of vocational rehabilitation, welfare of various kinds, and educational matters has increased steadily. The roles of state departments of vocational rehabilitation, post-secondary educational institutions, mental-health services, and the like are of increasing significance to the deaf. It is not necessary to document the degree and kind of service, nor even whether experts concur on the adequacy of these services. We take this growth to be self-evident. Our purpose is to theorize about the meaning of this expanded governmental role and its potential consequences for the deaf community.

Some activists suggest that the government seems to be capable of underwriting the continued existence of the deaf community through grants in aid and seed-money programs for starting awareness or resource centers, educational programs, and the like. However, the experiences of certain urban-based communities, such as blacks, inform us about the actual consequences of massive welfare spending. Martin and Martin (1978) document the existence of what they call the "extended family" among poor, urban, black people. They cogently argue that this network of "multigenerational, interdependent kinship system" functions as a "mutual aid system" for the welfare and survival of members of the larger urban black community (1978, p. 1). However, they describe a wholesale abandonment of the "extended family without the economic, political, or educational backgrounds" among the members of the community to form stable nuclear families. They attribute these tendencies to the welfare system itself. Although welfare aid may surely be necessary for survival, it forces the extended-family member to depend on government services. Subsequently, the black community relinquishes control over extended-family life to outsiders (Martin and Martin 1978, p. 87). Martin and Martin contend that welfare policies encourage black people to form nuclear families and that these policies do stress mainstream values of "work" while making the act of applying for welfare degrading. On the one hand, members of extended families are dissuaded from full utilization of the funds available; on the other hand, the actual funds provide scanty grants insufficient to allow poor blacks to break their dependence on the extended family (Martin and Martin 1978, p. 88).

Although scholars disagree about the precise effects of government involvement on the private lives of minority-community members, these same academics are quick to point out that the consequences of government policy are often unintended and may have negative effects on the structure of community life.

Historically, the deaf have been conservative in their stance toward "handouts" from the government. This posture is no doubt tied up with the normalization processes. Be that as it may, Gallaudet College is as close to a "national" college as any institution of higher learning in the United States. Most interpreting and, to be sure, the very possibility of a profession of interpreters, is directly attributable to government subsidies of educational, medical, and vocational services for the deaf.

The government seems to function in the deaf community as a surrogate parent. In the absence of other institutional supports from the private sector, the government responds. Unlike other more-primary or private social forms, however, the government acts as a bureaucracy. It does not integrate its programs for the development of the "total person." It is segmentalized and, as Weber pointed out about all bureaucracies, without an underlying humanistic philosophy. As we have learned generally, formal organizations reflect the dominant values of society. Hence, to the degree that the deaf community embodies values counter to those of the mainstream (negative attitudes toward English, adapted versions of success themes, and the neutralization of stigmatization) government involvement may be reasonably expected to undercut the very heart of the community. This is precisely Martin and Martin's point with regard to the black extended family.

The Image of Stability

In writing about how the deaf adapt to old age, Becker (1980) lists the symbolic nature of community as part of the larger pattern of coping skills she found among the aged deaf. She writes:

> Despite the cultural fragility of the deaf community, for example, the paucity of such common institutional supports as kin and ethnicity, it has continuity across generations. The aged deaf share a collective identity with all other deaf people. Their collective identity is based on a status devalued by inability. They have legitimized their status in their own eyes through a normalization process. [1980, p. 107]

Jacobs portrays the deaf as resourceful adults who, with the aid of fellow bearers of the identity, cope against great odds to become full participants, full humans, and fully social. Indeed, when one becomes immersed in the literature of the deaf community, an image appears of that community as stable, remarkably tenacious, independent, and above all vital. Membership in this community seems to provide for the deaf an insulation against childhood problems of impulsivity (Meadow 1980); against learning disabilities (Meadow 1980; Moores 1978); and against the uncertainty and pathos of old age (Becker 1980).

No researcher claims that the deaf community is a utopia. But, compared to the anomie, alienation, and pretension that some authors attribute to general society, the group life of the deaf seems an attractive alternative, an oasis in the desert. Years ago Best (1943) dedicated his book on the deaf to "the most misunderstood among the sons of men, but the 'gamest' of them all." The image of the deaf community that its members espouse, and the one that researchers closest to it reflect, is that the only problems that deaf people experience above and beyond those of everyday life are the result of having to deal with hearing people—their prejudices, their "English," and their unwillingness to treat the deaf as ordinary people (see Jacobs 1974). This image, of course, is consistent with the interests of the community itself. Although not thoroughly traditional, the deaf community does seem to manifest elements of a stable, viable symbolic community. Like that of other such communities, its very vitality is linked to core values that its members must protect. Especially apt at protecting these values and conveying them to outsiders in positive terms are long-time self-identified community members.

The contacts with outsiders that are unavoidable and the varied backgrounds of the members themselves shape deaf interactions into those of a small community like those studied by Albert Hunter. Hunter writes that such communities define interactional channels "within highly segmented roles and formally organized groups [resulting in] institutional and functional differentiation [which causes] the small community to lose its ability to meet the daily life needs of its residents" (Hunter 1974, p. 16).

The deaf community has been able to meet the life needs of its members only under unusual historical and organizational circumstances—for example, in the eighteenth century on Martha's Vineyard (Groce 1980); or at Gallaudet College or residential schools for the deaf when those institutions maintained farms and craft shops and were almost self-sufficient entities. It is from the image of the deaf community as a historical entity that the disposition to see it as positive derives. Although elements of this earlier "folk" state persist, the deaf community has been subject to the same changes that have affected all society.

Societal Change

The jury is still out on the full impact of the variegated and potent forces that buffet our society. Although Parsons's descriptions of modern qualitative features of action certainly have the ring of accuracy, other narrower and more-focused analyses have refined our understanding of urban society as the setting for everyday life (Irwin 1977; Goffman 1971; Hunter 1974). In the last section of this chapter, we want to explicate the consequences for the deaf community of various trends of modern society.

The "ideology of the individual" and its recent manifestations in the search for self-actualization have obvious implications for the solidarity of the deaf community. As the deaf achieve more participation in mainstream society, as they succeed in becoming more "ordinary," they will discover, as did traditionalists before them, that the motivational systems of modern people, the psychology appropriate to participation, often mitigate a strong sense of collective identity. Although one may "find oneself" in the context of a group experience, such as involvement in a religious cult, this discovery is interpreted from the perspective of ego, of the individual. The group is a medium, an instrument for the innerward journey through the self. Ironically, the strength of the deaf experience, its insulative function is due in part to the compensating effect one derives from participating fully in it, compared with the incomplete socialization a deaf person experiences in hearing society. It is not being able to participate normally in mainstream society that gives the community its appeal and efficacy in defining the selfhood of its members.

Selfhood is an individual rather than a collective matter in modern society. Individual identity or personal integration comes increasingly at the cost of collective solidarity. Instead of communities of contiguity, we see specific groups dedicated to the pursuit of specific interests, into and out of which individuals move. Irwin (1977) refers to these kinds of "communities" as *scenes.*

As people learn to use their associations for mutual benefit, they must learn self-control. Modern self-control is less the "self-discipline" of the past than the ability to gauge one's own needs and tolerances, to know when one has "had enough" or when one has exploited a group to its fullest extent. An encounter with a self-help, popular psychology group is beneficial, up to a point; spending energies in leisure-time activities is "healthy," up to a point; and aspiring to financial success "makes sense" only in terms of individually defined goals. "Health, happiness, and the pursuit of self" is the new motto for participation in society. Several sociologists have suggested that the structures of society, the new "waves" of social order, require a new type of person, and that we are seeing this new character emerge and mature. She or he is neither the Protestant worker of the industrial era nor the conformist of the social ethic (Whyte 1956). This creature is inwardly oriented but without the constraints of absolutist moral standards. He or she is sensitive to the social environment, but in a self-controlled manner. Group involvement and commitment, come only through reciprocally defined and mutually beneficial outcomes. The "personality" requires a great deal of "budgeted rationality" and managed emotions.

A corollary to the managed feelings and instrumental involvements of this citizen of the "new age" is the quest for independence. Consistent with Durkheim's vision of increased functional interdependence, the quest for an individual sense of independence has been redoubled. Sociologically, each of us depends on others in society to a far greater extent and in much more complex and interlinked patterns than at any other period in our history. Psychologically, we demand more control over ourselves; we guard our privacy tenaciously and "hole up" in the sanctity of our selfhood. Interdependence seems to us an inappropriate criterion for assessing our maturity, whereas psychological independence is seen as requiring constant work and development. Hence, parents attempt to encourage their children toward "independence," which means being accustomed to long periods of separation, learning to care for oneself, and generally acquiring the ability to internalize feelings and stifle urges to remain within the supportive and insulative environment of home and friends. Children are prepared to make it in the outside world, a world populated by strangers, manipulators, and essentially untrustworthy types.

The deaf community functions to increase the dependence of its members on one another. As emotional stakes are raised, as conformity to values is achieved within the community, the deaf person becomes a member of a collective entity quite unlike the foregoing characterization of the "real world." Obviously, to the degree that that member learns not simply to cope with but to be a part of that outside world, he or she becomes less able to achieve selfhood through immersion in group life. As Durkheim would have put it, egoism opposes altruism. The hearing world, with its egoistic definitions of social life, conflicts with the altruism of the deaf community.

The jobs that the deaf hold, those occupations that are available to them, reflect societal trends toward interdependence. New occupational pursuits have proliferated, largely in the areas of service, high technology, and information.

Benderly (1980) cites evidence that at the beginning of the twentieth century, the difference between the annual income of the deaf man's family and that of a hearing man's was insignificant. At a time when most people were artisans, manual laborers, or farmers, the deaf man or woman was able to achieve a reasonable assimilation into the "underclasses" of society. However, urbanization and the increased specialization of work has created more white-collar jobs. Essentially, these new jobs may be thought of as "information" jobs. They deal in various ways with telling about something, organizing or processing something. Perhaps the epitome of this new type of job is that of the consultant, who really does no direct production. Such occupations place a premium on communication and on the "presentation of self" (see Goffman 1959).

The presentation of self, the staging of everyday life, implies that language is used as performance. So strong is the emphasis in modern society on staging one's identity and acting out parts in order to achieve a desired end that Irwin (1977) suggests that the metaphor of life as drama has become literal. Our family and personal lives are backstages where we "dress up," "rehearse," and prepare to go out into the world. Irwin writes that this play acting entails consciousness.

> The fundamental dimension of acting in ordinary life routines is being conscious of oneself in the presence of others. A second feature, corollary to this fundamental aspect is that individuals, when on, construct action with the intention of conveying certain impressions about themselves, although they may have other aims as well. A third dimension is . . . that individuals remain aware that they have levels of existence apart from the self they are presenting in a particular setting. [Irwin 1977, p. 195]

We are aware of the requirements of drama, and we cultivate the facility with which to seek the roles best suited to our talents. Implied in this modern character are communicative élan and versatility. The mass media reinforce the dramaturgy; provide models; and help to set and disseminate trends in fashion, thought, and speech. Films and television, principally, mirror our activities and in the process deplete them. Role after role, scene after scene, the urban cowboy, the disco dancer, the self-actualizing housewife, the biker, the runner, the trucker parade before us, helping us to sharpen our own repertoires.

With the advent of captioned movies and television, in particular, more and more media fare become available to deaf people. The culture of the deaf provides the wherewithal for the interpretation of these data. Deaf playwrights and movie makers parody horror shows and struggle to elevate deaf lore to a literary form, often through the use of the best media technology. The impact of these dramas of everyday life is to accent the "egoism" of the modern social order. In order to act in a self-conscious fashion, one must possess the cognitive ability to impose one identity over another. As recent ethnographic work aptly demonstrates, the deaf community provides its members with a master identity. This identity gives rise to a core-self attribute that mediates all other role performances. To the extent that Irwin is correct about the scene-like character of modern society, master identities play increasingly less-salient roles in the quality of everyday performances. To the modern character, what one really *is* portends less of one's potential spoils of success than what one *can become*. An identity that is collectively defined, that is taken seriously, and that organizes whole segments of life activities into patterns seems quaint. To the degree that the deaf can acquire a modern character, their community will lessen in its sway over defining the quality of performances; its ability to provide the primary function of insulation will diminish correspondingly.

Positive consequences for the deaf community accrue from some general societal trends. For instance, in modern society there is a marked increase of tolerance and plurality, at least in public policy. As minority groups achieve recognition and expanded rights, the deaf will surely profit. To the extent that deaf activists are successful in drawing the analogy between their community and other subcultural groupings, deaf people will discover expanded opportunities in services and employment. There can be little doubt that deafness as a topic has received increased media attention. A number of popular books (Greenberg, *In This Sign*, New York: Avon Books, 1970; Spradley and Spradley, *Deaf Like Me*, New York: Random House, 1978; Benderly, *Dancing Without Music*) television shows ("My Name is Jonah"); and movies ("Voices") have all contributed to an appreciation of deafness among media audiences.

The backward glance of modern consciousness, its ability to use the past as nostalgia, has made collective experiences seem less alien and more appealing (Davis 1979). The general search for community in society gives alternative life-styles an allure. The deaf culture seems to have a freedom about it. It is there for the learning. To those willing to conform to its rules, it offers a feeling of identity separate from the stigmatization of the outside world. It has the appeal of a "movement" to some hearing people who study and know it. But as the deaf are discovered, they are also consumed by the modern society. The community itself becomes another scene in which actors play out segmentalized identities.

On balance, modernization seems to have more dysfunctional than functional effects on the deaf community. The net effect of full participation in society would be to render the community unnecessary, since its primary functions are adaptive. As long as there are people who must use a visual language, however, there will be a deaf community. But this community will continue to be shaped by larger societal forces. The shaping will result in a frame within which the meanings of deafness will emerge, and this frame can be anticipated.

Modern deaf people will alter the community they find. As enhanced social status is sought for the community, ties among members will be transformed; we can expect the deaf to suffer a sense of "homelessness" not unlike that of second-generation immigrants. Involvement among deaf people will become more instrumentally defined, and deaf culture may take on the flavor of a special-interest group.

As a special-interest group, deaf people will enter into competition with other groups and will move, with success, into greater dependence on the welfare state or the rehabilitative predilections of large corporations. Of course, this dependence will be coupled with greater egoism. The transition to dependence on the structure of modern society seems to be coming through a truncated process. In Western society the usual process leading to a collective form has been from individualism to individuation, a process bolstered by myths of self-determinancy and self-reliance. But the deaf community is moving into modern society without the benefits of any preparatory stages.

Movement from traditional to modern social structures can be accomplished swiftly, but there are hidden costs to a group of people whose principal adaptation to a handicap is sociolinguistic.

Bibliography

Alston, Ron. 1975. "Review of the Polls: Three Measures of Current Levels of Religiosity," *Journal for the Scientific Study of Religion* 14 (January): 165-168.

Baker, Charlotte, and Padden, Carol. 1978. "Language as a Multi-Channel Communication System." In *Understanding Language through Sign Language Research*, ed. P. Siple. New York: Academic Press.

Battison, Robbin. 1978. *Lexical Borrowing in American Sign Language.* Silver Springs, Md.: Linstok Press.

Becker, Gaylene. 1978. "Face to Face: Adaptive Responses to Disability and Old Age Among Deaf People." Ph.D. dissertation, University of California, San Francisco/Berkeley.

_____. 1980. *Growing Old in Silence.* Berkeley, Calif.: University of California Press.

Benderly, Beryl Lieff. 1980. *Dancing Without Music: Deafness in America.* Garden City, N.Y.: Doubleday.

Bensman, Joseph, and Vidich, Arthur. 1971. "The New Class System and Its Life Styles." In *The New American Society,* ed. J.Bensman and A.Vidich, pp. 139-157. New York: Quadrangle.

Berger, Peter. 1968. *The Sacred Canopy.* Garden City, N.Y.: Doubleday.

Berger, Peter, and Berger, Brigitte. 1972. *Sociology: A Biographical Approach.* New York: Basic Books.

Berger, Peter; Berger, Brigitte; and Kellner, Hansfried. 1973. *The Homeless Mind.* New York: Vintage Books.

Berger, Peter, and Kellner, Hansfried. 1964. "Marriage and the Construction of Reality." *Diogenes* 45:1-25.

Berger, Peter, and Luckmann, Thomas. 1967. *The Social Construction of Reality.* Garden City, N.Y.: Doubleday.

Bernstein, Basil. 1971. *Class, Codes and Control,* vol. 1. London: Routledge, Kegan Paul.

_____. 1972. "Social Class, Language and Socialization." In *Language and Social Context,* ed. P. Gigliol: pp. 157-178. Baltimore, Md.: Penguin.

Bernstein, Basil, and Henderson, Dorothy. 1969. "Social Class Differences in the Relevance of Language to Socialization." *Sociology* 3:1-20.

Best, Harry. 1943. *Deafness and the Deaf in the United States.* New York: Macmillan.

Bogardus, Emory. 1925. "Measuring Social Distance." *Journal of Applied Sociology* 9:299-308.

Brown, R., and Bellugi, U. 1964. "Three Processes in the Child's Acquisition of Syntax." In *New Directions in the Study of Language*, ed. Lenneberg, pp. 131-161. Cambridge, Mass.: MIT Press.

Cicourel, Aaron. 1970. "Basic and Normative Rules in the Negotiation of Status and Role." In *Recent Sociology*, no. 2, ed. Hans Peter Dreitzel, pp. 4-45. New York: Macmillan.

_____. 1974a. *Cognitive Sociology: Language and Meaning in Social Interaction.* New York: Free Press.

_____. 1974b. "Gestural Sign Language and the Study of Nonverbal Communication." *Sign Language Studies* 4:35-76.

_____. 1974c. *Theory and Method in a Study of Argentine Fertility.* New York: Wiley.

Circourel, Aaron, and Boese, Robert J. 1972. "Sign Language Acquisition and the Teaching of Deaf Children." In *Functions of Language in the Classroom,* ed. C.B. Cazden, V.P. John, and D. Hymes, pp. 32-62. New York: Teachers College Press.

Colman, R.F., and Neugarten, B.L. 1971. *Social Status in the City.* San Francisco, Calif.: Jossey-Bass.

Cook-Gumperz, Jenny. 1975. "The Child as Practical Reasoner." In *Sociocultural Dimensions of Language Use,* ed. M. Sanches and B.G. Blount, pp. 137-162. New York: Academic Press.

Coser, Lewis. 1956. *Functions of Social Conflict.* London: Free Press.

Crammatte, Allen B. 1968. *Deaf Persons in Professional Employment.* Springfield, Ill.: Charles C. Thomas.

Cuddihy, John Murray. 1974. *The Ordeal of Civility.* New York: Delta.

Curtis, James M. 1978. *Culture as Polyphony.* Columbia: University of Missouri Press.

Curtiss, Susan. 1977. *Genie: A Psycholinguistic Study of a Modern-Day "Wild Child."* New York: Academic Press.

Davis, Fred. 1979. *Yearning for Yesterday: A Sociology of Nostalgia.* New York: Free Press.

Davis, Kingsley. 1959. "The Myth of Functional Analysis as a Special Method of Sociology and Antropology." *American Sociological Review* 10 (December):759.

Dawes, Alan. 1978. "Theories of Social Action." In *A History of Sociological Analysis,* ed. Tom Bottomore and Robert Nisbet, pp. 362-417. New York: Basic Books.

DeVillers, Peter, and DeVillers, Jill G. 1979. *Early Language.* Cambridge, Mass.: Harvard University Press.

Douglas, Jack D. 1976. *Investigative Social Research.* Beverly Hills, Calif.: Sage Publications.

Durkheim, Emile. 1938. *The Rules of the Sociological Method.* New York: Free Press.

Erting, Carol. 1978. "Language Policy and Deaf Ethnicity in the United States." *Sign Language Studies* 19:139-152.

_____. 1980. "Sign Language and Communication Between Adults and

Children." In *Sign Language and the Deaf Community,* ed. C. Baker and R. Battison, pp. 159–176. Silver Springs, Md: National Association of the Deaf.

Fant, Louie. 1972. *Ameslan: An Introduction to American Sign Language.* Silver Springs, Md: National Association of the Deaf.

Fishman, Joshua. 1970. *Sociolinguistics: A Brief Introduction.* Rowley, Mass.: Newbury House.

———. 1972. *Sociology of Language.* Rowley, Mass.: Newbury House.

Fromkin, V., and Rodman, R. 1978. *An Introduction to Language.* New York: Holt, Rinehart and Winston.

Furth, Hans. 1964. *Thinking Without Language.* New York: Free Press.

———. 1973. *Deafness and Learning: A Psychosocial Approach.* Belmont, Calif.: Wadsworth Publishing.

Garfinkel, Harold. 1967. *Studies in Ethnomethodology.* Englewood Cliffs, N.J.: Prentice-Hall.

Gans, Herbert J. 1962. *The Urban Villagers.* New York: Free Press.

Goffman, Erving. 1959. *The Presentation of Self in Everyday Life.* Garden City, N.Y.: Doubleday.

———. 1963. *Stigma: Notes of the Management of Spoiled Identity.* Englewood Cliffs, N.J.: Prentice-Hall.

———. 1971. *Relations in Public.* New York: Basic Books.

———. 1974. *Frame Analysis.* New York: Harper.

Gonos, George. 1977. " 'Situation' vs. 'Frame': The 'Interactionist' and the 'Structuralist' Analysis of Everyday Life." *American Sociological Review* 42 (December):854-867.

Goodwin, Charles. 1979. "The Interactive Construction of a Sentence in Natural Conversation." In *Everyday Language: Studies in Ethnomethodolgy* ed. George Psathas, pp. 97-121. New York: Irvington Publishers.

Goody, J., and Watt, I. 1972. "The Consequences of Literacy." In *Language and Social Context,* ed. P. Giglioli, pp. 311-357. Baltimore, Md: Penguin.

Gouldner, Alvin W. 1970. *The Coming Crisis of Western Sociology.* New York: Avon Books.

Gove, Walter. 1975. *The Labelling of Deviance.* New York: Halsted Press.

Grimshaw, Allen D. 1979. "Social Problems and Social Policies: An Illustration from Sociolinguistics." *Social Problems* 26(June):582-598.

Groce, Nora. 1980. "Everyone Here Spoke Sign Language." *Natural History* 89(June):10-16.

Gussow, Zachary, and Tracy, George S. 1971. "Status, Ideology and Adaptation to Stigmatized Illness." In *The Other Minorities,* ed. Edward Sagarin, pp. 242-262. Waltham, Mass.: Ginn and Company.

Haber, Lawrence D., and Smith, Richard T. 1971. "Disability and Deviance: Normative Adaptations of Role Behavior." *American Sociological Review* 36:87-97.

Habermas, Jürgen. 1970. "Toward a Theory of Communicative Competency." In *Recent Sociology*, no. 2, ed. Hans Peter Dreitzel, pp. 115-148. New York: Macmillan.

Hall, Robert A. 1955. *Hands Off Pidgin English.* New South Wales: Pacific Publications.

Hewitt, John P. 1976. *Self and Society: A Symbolic Interactionist Social Psychology.* Boston: Allyn and Bacon.

Higgins, Paul C. 1977. "The Deaf Community: Identity and Interaction in a Hearing World." Ph.D. dissertation, Northwestern University.

_____. 1979a. "Outsiders in a Hearing World: The Deaf Community." *Urban Life* 8(April):3-22.

_____. 1979b. "Deviance within a Disabled Community: Peddling Among the Deaf." *Pacific Sociological Review* 22(January):96-114.

_____. 1980a. *Outsiders in a Hearing World: A Sociology of Deafness.* Beverly Hills, Calif.: Sage Publications.

_____. 1980b. "Societal Reaction and the Physically Disabled: Bringing the Impairment Back." *Symbolic Interaction* 3(Spring):139-156.

Hummel, Ralph P. 1978. *The Bureaucratic Experience.* New York: St. Martin's.

Hunter, Albert. 1974. *Symbolic Communities: The Persistence and Change of Chicago's Local Community.* Chicago: University of Chicago Press.

Hyman, Herbert H. 1953. "The Value Systems of Different Classes." In *Class, Status and Power*, ed. R. Bendix and S.M. Lipset, pp. 488-499. New York: Free Press.

Irwin, John. 1977. *Scenes.* Beverly Hills, Calif.: Sage Publications.

Jacobs, Leo M. 1974. *A Deaf Adult Speaks Out.* Washington, D.C.: Gallaudet College Press.

Joos, Martin. 1961. *The Five Clocks.* New York: Harbinger Books.

Keyes, Ralph. 1973. *We, the Lonely People: Searching for Community.* New York: Harper and Row.

Kingsley, Davis. 1959. "The Myth of Functional Analysis as a Special Method of Sociology." *American Sociological Review* 10(December):757-772.

Klima, E., and Bellugi, U. 1979. *The Signs of Language.* Cambridge, Mass.: Harvard University Press.

Kruger, Susan. 1979. *Hip Capitalism.* Beverly Hills, Calif.: Sage Publications.

Labov, William. 1970. "The Logic of Nonstandard English." In *Language and Poverty*, ed. F. Williams, pp. 153-189. Chicago: Markham Publishing Company.

_____. 1972. "The Study of Language in Its Social Context." In *Language and Social Context*, ed. P. Giglioli, pp. 283-307. Baltimore, Md.: Penguin.

_____. 1974. "The Art of Sounding and Signifying." In *Language in Its Social Setting*, ed. William Gage, pp. 84-116. Washington, D.C.: Antropological Association of Washington.

Lawton, Dennis. 1968. *Social Class, Language and Education*. New York: Schocken Books.

Leiter, Kenneth. 1980. *A Primer on Ethnomethodology*. New York: Oxford University Press.

Le Masters, E.E. 1975. *Blue-Collar Aristocrats*. Madison: University of Wisconsin Press.

Lieberman, T. 1975. *On the Origins of Language*. New York: Macmillan.

Lofland, John. 1976. *Doing Social Life: The Qualitative Study of Human Interaction in Natural Settings*. New York: Wiley Interscience.

_____. 1978. *Doomsday Cult*. New York: Irvington.

Luckmann, Benita. 1978. "The Small Life-Worlds of Modern Man." In *Phenomenology and Sociology*, ed. T. Luckmann, pp. 275-290. New York: Penguin.

Lunde, Anders. 1956. "The Sociology of the Deaf." Paper presented at the meetings of the American Sociological Association, Detroit, Mich.

Lyman, Stanford, and Scott, Marvin. 1970. *A Sociology of the Absurd*. New York: Appleton-Century-Crofts.

Lynd, Robert S., and Lynd, Helen Merrell. 1929. *Middletown*. New York: Harcourt, Brace and World.

Manning, Peter K., and Fabrega, Horacio, Jr. 1973. "The Experience of Self and Body: Health and Illness in the Chicago Highlands." In *Phenomenological Sociology: Issues and Applications*. ed. G. Psathas, pp. 251-301. New York: Wiley.

Markowicz, Harry. 1972. "Some Sociolinguistic Considerations of American Sign Language." *Sign Language Studies* 1:15-41.

_____. 1974. "Sign English: Is It Really English?" Linguistic Research Laboratory, Gallaudet College, Washington, D.C. Mimeographed.

Martin, E.P., and Martin, J.M. 1978. *The Black Extended Family*. Chicago: University of Chicago Press.

Matza, David. 1964. *Delinquency and Drift*. New York: Wiley.

McHugh, Peter. 1970. "A Common Sense Perception of Deviance." In *Recent Sociology*, no. 2, ed. Hans Peter Dreitzel, pp. 152-180. New York: Macmillan.

McKinney, John C. 1970. "Sociological Theory and the Process of Typification." In *Theoretical Sociology: Perspectives and Development*, ed. J.C. McKinney and E. A. Tiryakian, pp. 235-269. New York: Appleton-Century-Crofts.

McNeill, David. 1966. "Developmental Psycholinguistics." In *Genesis of Language*, ed. F. Smith and G. Miller, pp. 15-84. Cambridge, Mass.: MIT Press.

Mead, G.H. 1934. *Mind, Self and Society*. Chicago: University of Chicago Press.

Meadow, Kathryn P. 1968. "Parental Responses to the Medical Ambiguities of Deafness." *Journal of Health and Social Behavior* 9:299-309.

————. 1969. "Self Image, Family Climate and Deafness." *Social Forces* 47: 428-438.

————. 1972. "Sociolinguistics, Sign Language and the Deaf Subculture." In *Psycholinguistics and Total Communication: The State of the Art,* ed. T.J. O'Rourke, pp. 19-37. Washington, D.C.: American Annuals of the Deaf.

————. 1977. "Name Signs as Identity Symbols in the Deaf Community." *Sign Language Studies* 16:237-246.

————. 1980. *Deafness and Child Development.* Berkeley: University of California Press.

Meadow, Kathryn P., and Nemon, A. 1976. "Deafness as Stigma." *American Rehabilitation* 2:7-9, 19-22.

Mehan, Hugh, and Wood, Houston. 1975. *The Reality of Ethnomethodology.* New York: Wiley.

Merton, Robert K. 1963. *Social Theory and Social Structure.* Glencoe, Ill.: Free Press.

————. 1974. *Sociological Ambivalence and Other Essays.* New York: Free Press.

Mills, C. Wright. 1951. *White Collar.* New York: Oxford University Press.

————. 1959. *The Sociological Imagination.* New York: Oxford University Press.

Montgomery, George. 1978. *Of Sound and Mind.* Edinburgh: Scottish Workshop Publications.

Moore, Wilbert E. 1978. "Functionalism." In *A History of Sociological Analysis,* ed. Tom Bottomore and Robert Nisbet, pp. 321-361. New York: Basic Books.

Moores, Donald F. 1978. *Educating the Deaf: Psychology, Principles and Practices.* Boston, Mass.: Houghton Mifflin Company.

Morris, Monica. 1977. *An Excursion into Creative Sociology.* New York: Columbia University Press.

Nash, Anedith. 1976. "Observation in a Bilingual Classroom: The Role of the Interpreter." In *Sociology: A Descriptive Approach*, ed. J.E. Nash and J.P. Spradley, pp. 388-403. Chicago: Rand McNally.

Nisbet, Robert. 1973. *The Social Philosophers: Community and Conflic: in Western Thought.* New York: Thomas Y. Crowell Company.

O'Neill, John. 1973. "Embodiment and Child Development: A Phenomenoligical Approach." In *Childhood and Socialization,* ed. Hans Peter Dreitzel, pp. 65-81. New York: Macmillian.

Padden, Carol. 1980. "The Deaf Community and the Culture of Deaf People." In *Sign Language and the Deaf Community,* ed. C. Baker and R. Battison, pp. 80-103. Silver Springs, Md: National Association of the Deaf.

Padden, Carol, and Markowicz, Harry. 1976. "Cultural Conflicts Between Hearing and Deaf Communities." *Proceedings of the Seventh World Congress of the World Federation of the Deaf.* Silver Springs, Md: National Association of the Deaf.

Parker, Bill. 1973. "Cultural Variables and the Black Experience." Educational Testing Service, Princeton, N.J. Mimeographed.

Parsons, Talcott. 1937. *The Structure of Social Action.* New York: McGraw-Hill.

_____. 1951. *Toward a General Theory of Action.* New York: Harper and Row.

_____. 1966. *Societies: Evolutionary and Comparative Perspectives.* Englewood Cliffs, N.J.: Prentice-Hall.

_____. 1971. *The System of Modern Societies.* Englewood Cliffs, N.J.: Prentice-Hall.

Parsons, Talcott; Bales, Robert F.; and Shils, Edward A. 1953. *Working Papers in the Theory of Action.* New York: Free Press.

Peng, Fred. 1977. "Sign Language and Culture." *Sociolinguistics Newsletter* 8 (Spring):28-29.

Pfuetze, Paul E. 1954. *The Social Self.* New York: Bookman.

Psathas, George. 1968. "Ethnomethods and Phenomenology." *Social Research* 35:500-520.

_____. 1973. *Phenomenological Sociology: Issues and Applications.* New York: Wiley.

_____. 1979. *Everyday Language: Studies in Ethnomethodology.* New York: Irvington Publishers.

Rainwater, Lee. 1966. "Fear and the House-as-Haven in the Lower Class." *Journal of the American Institute of Planners* 32(January):23-31.

_____. 1974. *What Money Buys: Inequality and the Social Meanings of Income.* New York: Basic Books.

Reilly, Judy, and McIntire, Marina L. 1980. "American Sign Language and Pidgin Sign English: What's the Difference?" *Sign Language Studies* 27: 151-192.

Robinson, W.P., and Rackstraw, S.J. 1972. *A Question of Answers,* vols. I and II. London: Routledge, Kegan Paul.

Rodman, H. 1963. "The Lower Class Value Stretch." *Social Forces* 42:205-215.

Sacks, Harvey. 1972. "An Initial Investigation of the Usability of Conversational Data for Doing Sociology." In *Studies in Social Interaction,* ed. David Sudow, pp. 31-74. New York: Free Press.

Schein, Jerome D. 1968. *The Deaf Community: Studies in Social Psychology of Deafness.* Washington, D.C.: Gallaudet College Press.

Schein, Jerome D. and Delk, M.T., Jr. 1974. *The Deaf Population of the United States.* Silver Springs, Md: National Association of the Deaf.

Schlesinger, Hilde S., and Meadow, Kathryn P. 1972. *Sound and Sign: Childhood Deafness and Mental Health.* Berkeley: University of California Press.

Schutz, Alfred. 1962. *Collected Papers,* vol. I. The Hague: Martinus Nijhoff.

_____. 1971. *Collected Papers,* vol. II. The Hague: Martinus Nijhoff.

Scott, David. 1978. "Stigma in and about the Deaf Community." In *Deafness,*

Personality and Mental Health, ed. George Montgomery, pp. 21-29. Eding-burgh: Scottish Workshop Publications.

Scott, Marvin, and Lyman, Stanford. 1968. "Accounts." *American Sociological Review* 33:46-62.

Seeman, Melvin. 1956. "Intellectual Perspective and Adjustment to Minority Status." *Social Problems* 3:142-153.

Sherohman, James. 1977. "Conceptual and Methodological Issues in the Study of Role Taking Accuracy." *Symbolic Interaction,* Fall, pp. 121-131.

Shuy, Roger W., and Fasold, Ralph W., eds. 1973. *Language Attitudes: Current Trends and Prospects.* Washington, D.C.: Georgetown University Press.

Siple, Patricia. 1978. "Visual Constraints for Sign Language Communication." *Sign Language Studies* 19:95-110.

Smith, Richard T. 1975. "Societal Reaction and Physical Disability: Contrasting Perspectives." In *The Labelling of Deviance,* ed. Walter R. Gove, pp. 147-156. New York: Wiley.

Spradley, James P. 1971. *You Owe Yourself a Drunk.* Boston: Little, Brown.

——. 1972. *Culture and Cognition: Rules, Maps and Plans.* San Francisco: Chandler.

——. 1979. *The Ethnographic Interview.* New York: Holt, Rinehart and Winston.

Spradley, James P., and Mann, Brenda J. 1975. *Cocktail Waitress: Woman's Work in a Man's World.* New York: Wiley.

Stack, Carol. 1974. *All Our Kin.* New York: Harper and Row.

Stevens, K., and House, A. 1955. "Development of a Quantitative Description of Vowel Articulation." *Journal of the Acoustical Society of America* 27: 484-493.

Steward, William. 1968. "A Sociolinguistic Typology for Describing National Multi-lingualism." *Readings in the Sociology of Language,* ed. J. Fishman, p. 531. The Hague: Mouton.

Stonequist, E.V. 1937. *The Marginal Man.* New York: Scribner.

Stokes, Randall, and Hewitt, John P. 1976. "Aligning Action." *American Sociological Review* 41 (October):838-849.

Stokoe, William C. 1970. "Sign Language Diglossia." *Studies in Linguistics* 21:24-41.

——. 1978. *Sign Language Structure* [1960]. Silver Springs, Md: Linstok Press.

——. 1980. "The Study and the Use of Sign Language." In *Nonspeech Language and Communication,* ed. Richard L. Shiefelbusch, pp. 125-155. Baltimore, Md.: University Park Press.

Stokoe, William C., and Kuschel, Rolf. 1979. *A Field Guide for Sign Language Research.* Silver Springs, Md: Linstok Press.

Stokoe, William C.; Bernard, H. Russell; and Padden, Carol. 1976. "An Elite Group in Deaf Society." *Sign Language Studies* 12(Fall):189-210.

Strauss, Anselm. 1978. *Negotiations: Varieties, Contexts, Processes and Social Order*. San Francisco: Jossey-Bass.

Sturtevant, William C. 1967. "Studies in Ethnoscience." *American Anthropologist* 66(June):99-131.

Sudnow, David. 1965. "Normal Crime." *Social Problems* 12:255-276.

Sussman, Marvin. 1965. "Sociological Theory and Deafness." Proceedings of a National Research Conference on Behavioral Aspects of Deafness, New Orleans, La.

Sykes, Gresham M., and Matza, David. 1957. "Techniques of Neutralization." *American Sociological Review* 22:667-69.

Talese, Gay. 1980. *Thy Neighbor's Wife*. Garden City, N.Y.: Doubleday.

Taylor, Orlando L. 1973. "Teachers' Attitudes Toward Black and Nonstandard English as Measured by the Language Attitude Scale." In *Language Attitudes: Current Trends and Prospects*, ed. Roger Shuy and Ralph W. Fasold, pp. 174-201. Washington, D.C.: Georgetown University Press.

Tiryakian, Edward A. 1965. "Existential Phenomenology and Sociological Tradition." *American Sociological Review* 30(October):674-688.

Toufler, Alvin. 1980. *The Third Wave*. New York: William Morrow and Company.

Trudgill, Peter. 1974. *Sociolinguistics: An Introduction*. Baltimore, Md: Penguin Books.

Trybus, Raymond J., ed. 1977. "Mental Health in Deafness." Proceedings of the First Orthopsychiatric Workshop on Deafness. Washington, D.C.

Turner, Jonathan H. 1978. *The Structure of Sociological Theory*, rev. ed. Homewood, Ill: Dorsey Press.

Turner, Jonathan H., and Maryanski, Alexandria. 1979. *Functionalism*. Mento Park, Calif.: Benjamin Cummings Publishing Company.

Turner, Roy. 1970. "Words, Utterance and Activities." In *Understanding Everyday Life* ed. J.D. Douglas, pp. 169-187. Chicago: Aldine.

Uden, A. Van. 1968. *A World of Language for Deaf Children*, part I: *Basic Principles*. The Netherlands: St. Michielsgestel.

Useem, Ruth, and Gibson, Duane L. 1960. "The Function of Neighboring for the Middle Class Male." *Human Organization* 19(Summer):68-76.

Vernon, McKay, and Makowsky, Bernard. 1969. "Deafness and Minority Group Dynamics." *The Deaf American*, July-August, pp. 3-6.

Wagner, Helmut R. 1970. *Alfred Schutz on Phenomenology and Social Relations*. Chicago: University of Chicago Press.

Wallace, Ruth A., and Wolf, Alison. 1980. *Contemporary Sociological Theory*. Englewood Cliffs, N.J.: Prentice-Hall.

Warner, W. Lloyd. 1960. *Social Class in America*. New York: Harper and Row.

Watson, Douglas, ed. 1973. *Readings on Deafness*. New York: Deafness Research and Training Center.

Weigert, Andrew. 1975. "Alfred Schutz on a Theory of Motivation." *Pacific Sociological Review* 18 (January):83-102.

Whyte, William H., Jr. 1956. *The Organization Man.* Garden City, N.Y.: Doubleday.

Wilbur, Ronnie. 1979. *American Sign Language and Sign Systems.* Baltimore,
Md.: University Park Press.

Williams, Robin. 1970. *American Society*, 3d ed. New York: Alfred Knopf.

Woodward, James C. 1972. "Implications for Sociolinguistics Research Among
the Deaf." *Sign Language Studies* 1:1-7.

_____. 1973. "Some Characteristics of Pidgin Signed English." *Sign Language
Studies* 3:39-46.

_____. 1979. *Signs of Sexual Behavior.* Silver Springs, Md: T.J. Publishers.

Yinger, Milton. 1957. *Religion, Society and the Individual.* New York: Macmillan.

Zakarewsky, George T. 1979. "Patterns of Support Among Gay Lesbian Deaf
Persons." *Sexuality and Disability*, Fall, pp. 178-191.

Zaner, Richard, and Ihde, Don, eds. 1973. *Phenomenology and Existentialism.*
New York: Capricorn Books.

Zimmerman, Don. 1978. "Ethnomethodology." *American Sociologist* 13(Febru-
ary):6-15.

Index

About the Authors

Jeffrey E. Nash is an associate professor of sociology at Macalester College, Saint Paul, Minnesota. He received the Ph.D. from Washington State University in 1971 and has taught at the University of Tulsa. Professor Nash has researched several aspects of everyday life in modern society and is interested in the sociolinguistics of human interaction. He has published articles in journals such as *Journal of Psycholinguistics, Urban Life, Sociological Quarterly,* and *Qualitative Sociology.* He is currently studying the organization of teletypewriter conversations.

Anedith Nash is a Ph.D. candidate in the Program in American Studies, University of Minnesota. She teaches American studies and urban studies and has published articles in *Urban Life, Sign Language Studies,* and *Prospects.* Her current work includes a study of the New Deal's Federal Theatre Project.